AF597254

HERO

ABHISHEK
KRISHNAN

Notion Press

Old No. 38, New No. 6
McNichols Road, Chetpet
Chennai - 600 031

First Published by Superstar (An Imprint of Notion Press) 2018

ISBN 978-93-86295-08-8

Dedication

This book is dedicated to all passionate aspirants, who are looking to make it big someday.

Contents

Preface

Dear Readers,

This book is a journey
A collection of real life experiences,
A message to film aspirants,
A dedication to passion,
A celebration of friendship and love,
An excerpt from everyday life.

I welcome you all to *Hero*.

Acknowledgements

I thank my Mom and Dad for giving me life and thus bestowing upon me the opportunity to meet some wonderful people.

I thank Mydhili Mithra and Khushboo Mundhra for accompanying me on this journey, constantly nagging me to write and asking me what happens next.

I thank Saranya, Channi, Perinbanathan and Chalukyan for all their help during the initial stages of the novel.

I thank team Wizguys, for all the fun experiences we had in college.

I thank Perinbanathan for constantly torturing me with his boring love stories.

I thank Yogesh for listening to the narration of the entire story and making genuine attempts to help me.

I thank Manoj, Kaushik, Abishek, Dilani, Mithun, Sudharshan, Jyothsna, Tamil, Anita, Avinash and all my buddies at *Behindwoods.com* for constantly encouraging my writing.

A heart full of gratitude to Meera, Malu, Sandya and Suresh for their unconditional support and love.

I thank my ex-girlfriends for creating all the memorable moments, which helped me write this book.

I thank the team at Notion Press for helping me edit the manuscript and publish it.

I thank my friends and relatives for helping me bring this book to life.

Above all, I am grateful that I took this opportunity to expand my limits and work beyond my comfort zone.

Prologue

The rusty old gate creaked as I closed it behind me. My eyes were alarmingly red. I walked aimlessly in the busy streets of Coimbatore, letting my feet do the arduous task of steering my bone-weary body to safety. My feet found their way into a messy bar.

I ran my finger through the various choices on the menu card and stopped at 'whisky'. I turned to the impatient waiter.

"Teacher's. Large. On the rocks," I said.

The waiter drifted away after taking the order. I placed my hands on my head and rested on the table.

"Why me of all the people in the world?" I asked myself. "God, just let this time pass quickly."

The waiter placed the glass of whisky on the table. I grabbed the glass and sent the whisky down my oesophagus before the waiter could say *your drink, sir*.

"One more..." I ordered as the concentrated intoxicant hit my head making me squawk.

The waiter returned with a replacement only to see it go down my throat in a jiffy.

"One more please..." I demanded as a drop of sweat moistened my thick eyebrow.

The waiter widened his lips, forcing a manufactured smile.

"Sure sir...," he said and darted away.

I lifted my glass to gulp down my third peg when I felt someone stop me. The man held my hand and stared at me through his thick square-framed glasses. He had a round face and a French beard that matched his hefty appearance. I glared at the man, my deep red eyes intensifying my outrage.

"Who the hell are you?" I asked, the words slipping through my inebriated tongue.

"You are Abhishek, aren't you?" the man asked, meekly.

"Never answer a question with another question. You understand?" I fumed. "Now tell me. Who in the world are you?"

"*Eda pulle.* This is Renjith."

My eyes widened. This voice was very familiar. It had been quite a while since I heard someone swear at me in Malayalam, which was my mother tongue. I shook my head and tried to focus on the blurry round human in front of me.

"Bloody meat brain. How are you?" I asked stretching my arms wide and moving forward to give him a hug.

Friends, they just can't let go of a few habitual addictions. They have to use foul language at each other, and they have to give each other a hug when they meet after a long time.

Renjith was a good friend of mine. We happened to *kuppa kottify* in the same college for three years. That was when we were transformed from mere strangers to thick buddies. Life had different plans in store for us. We were forced to turn to different routes to follow our respective dreams.

"What has happened to you? You look all screwed up," said Renjith.

Tears filled my eyes. I held my friend's hand and broke down, sobbing.

• • •

Renjith waited patiently in front of his house after ringing the doorbell the third time. After what seemed like an hour, the door swung open. A young, attractive lady with long, wet hair that made her clothes wet and defined her sculpted waist stood at the doorway. The gentle breeze that blew past her carried the exquisite scent of Hamam soap.

"I'm sorry, I was taking a bath," she said.

Typically, Renjith would have taken her into the bedroom to open another chapter of their usual intercourse sessions. But his emotions were handcuffed by the perturbed guest he had brought home.

"Hello, Jesse. How are you?" I asked with a smile that expressed mixed feelings of worriment and warmth.

"Abbbi, is that you? I mean, how are you? What's with that beard? What has happened to you? You look awful."

I responded to the array of questions with an uncomfortable grin and glanced at Renjith. Jesse understood the situation and widened the door to let us in.

"I think you people need to freshen up," she said.

I found my way into the washroom while Renjith followed his wife into the kitchen. He hugged her from behind and gave her a little peck on her cheek.

"What's wrong with him? Is everything okay?" she enquired.

"I don't quite know. We've got to sit down for a little chat," he said.

I sat by the round glass dining table with Renjith and Jesse on either side of me.

"You want a drink?" Renjith asked.

"Whisky. On the rocks," I replied, without allowing even a slight pause between the question and the answer.

Renjith correlated himself with the waiter in the bar as he rose to fetch a bottle of whisky.

"So tell me. What is wrong?" Renjith asked as he dropped a cube of ice into the drink. "I never thought I would see you like this."

"Yes, you look terrible... and... God... when did you start drinking?" Jesse asked.

"What's wrong with you? Why are you upset? When did you come down to Coimbatore? How did you get here? What have you been doing all these years? What do you do now? Have you been crying?"

Prologue

The questions were shot at me in rapid succession. I sat staring at the intoxicant before me mutely. I stirred my whisky, sending the ice cubes rattling against the walls of the glass before being swirled into a whirlpool. My mind was just like the whirlpool. So many thoughts swirled around in my head forming never-ending orbits. I knew the answers to all the questions that were being fired at me. But I just did not know where to start. I gulped down my drink and walked to a window at the far end of the living room.

I stared at the silent night through the barriers of the window. To get the answers to all their questions, we had to break open the window. We had to snap out of our current systematic, materialistic lives and go back to our liberal, carefree days. We had to prepare for a journey back in time. I picked up an old alarm clock that was placed among the other proud antique gizmos in the bragging showcase. My thick lips managed a feeble smile that hid under my beard. I gently put my fingers on the hands of the alarm clock and whirled them backwards. My mind slowly uncoiled out of the whirlpool turning younger, clearer and luminant.

1

An Eventful Day at College

I woke up to the deafening sound of the alarm clock screeching at me. I sprang out of my cot, shooting my blanket onto the ceiling fan. I tumbled to the floor, eyes still closed and my hands on the table trying to get hold of the loudmouth that disrupted one of those rare erotic dreams I managed to have.

"I hate you. I hate you. I hate you," I murmured as I silenced the incriminated monster with a blow on its head.

My eyelids were forced apart after losing their last hopes of continuing the dream from where it got cut off because of the clock. It was a quarter past nine.

"What the bloody hell?" I barked. "Firstly, you shook me out of a rare dream, and then you make me realise that I have been woken up at the wrong time. Goddammit, I have to make it to college in fifteen minutes."

The alarm clock stood to face me with its handicapped hands wide apart, like Jesus Christ, taking all the arraignment and silently asking God to forgive me.

It's a funny world. Everyone hates being woken up by the alarm clock and yet they have to use it. Imagine being cursed for doing just the job you've been asked to do, and precisely on time. Well, that's the fate of an alarm clock. One of man's confusing inventions.

"Who fiddled with my alarm clock?" I yelled as I charged out of my room.

I was answered by a loud whistle that came from the steaming pressure cooker. My mother turned a deaf ear to my nettled interrogation. If she had stepped out of the kitchen in a ridiculous attempt to probe the issue, my sister and I would have had to have lunch in our respective school and college canteens. Veena, my sister, and quite evidently the culprit responsible for the drama, sat in a corner, staring at her physics book. She looked at me from the corner of her eyes pretending to be oblivious to the fact that such a thing as an alarm clock even existed in the history of the universe.

I hurried back into my room. I did not want to waste time playing Scotland Yard, especially when I knew that the people at home had swallowed a bottle of glue for breakfast. Moreover, there was no point. What was I going to do if I found out? I was still going to be late. I rushed out of my room before the pressure cooker could gather up steam to manage another whistle.

"Key, key, key... where the hell is my bike key?"

I hunted all over the house, my teeth half-brushed, my shirt hardly pressed and my hair pointing in different directions.

"What's the problem? What happened to your alarm clock?" my father enquired, as he blew into some steaming black tea in a steel tumbler.

I glanced at my watch after having found my bike key. I still had about seven seconds to spare. I looked at my dad hopelessly.

"*Acha*, that happened a year ago. Forget it."

"You kids. Where do you pick up so much sarcasm from? In our times we never dared to speak like this to our parents."

My father switched on his radio channel.

Veena plugged in her earphones and started listening to Radio Mirchi.

"I'm leaving," I yelled as I fiddled with my shoelaces.

"Aren't you having breakfast?" my mom asked.

"No *amma*, I am late already. We have our investiture ceremony today. I'll eat at Chalu's place. I might come back late. See you. Bye." I attached all these words into a zip file and sent it across to my mom.

"What about lunch?" my mother shouted out from behind as I disappeared out the door.

"Canteen," I replied, my sound waves losing decibels as they passed through the closed window.

My fingers galloped across my mobile phone as I rushed towards my bike.

Macha, I'm on my way. Sorry woke up late. Be ready, I'll be there in five minutes.

I sent the message to Chalu and whizzed away on my Honda Activa.

Chalukyan a.k.a Chalu was one of my childhood friends. He stayed just across the street from my house thereby earning ourselves the moniker 'area friends'. Both Chalu and I caught the creativity bug.

However, our areas of interests were very different. I was into acting, filmmaking and writing whereas Chalu was more into painting, sketching and graphic designing. We dug our talents out at a very young age and found our goals much before we entered college. Our ambitions drove us into taking up visual communication, as a major, after our schooling. Both of us got into the Masan Memorial College of Arts and Science and became college friends as well. We were in our final year now, and were steering our respective ships in the directions we fancied.

I wanted to become a noteworthy actor, whose immaculate skills would always be in the limelight. This profound passion crept into my blood when I was in high school. When the other students clogged up their brains studying circuits of machines and heartbeats of frogs, I closely observed the peerless expressions of Mohan Lal, Kamal Haasan, Amitabh Bachchan and Aamir Khan. My mirror would often fall victim to my incessant practice sessions, forced to witness my overflowing variety of whimsical expressions.

I steered through the traffic, glancing at my watch, counting every millisecond. I thought of those days in the past when I had to just ride across the street to get to Chalu's house. Now, thanks to the state's ambitious metro railway project, even the pedestrians had to walk at least a kilometre back and forth just to get across the road. After honking, pulling the brake suddenly and accelerating a zillion times, I got to the other side of the road. I galloped up the stairs that led to Chalu's apartment and pushed open the door gasping for breath.

"*Macha*, come fast. We're late already," I said as I stepped in.

When my eyes adjusted themselves to the interiors of his house, I noticed my good old friend, sitting on the couch, wearing nothing except a towel wrapped around his waist. He was leisurely reading the newspaper, sipping a cup of coffee, as though he had just woken up after practising an exotic session of Kama Sutra during a honeymoon.

"Perfect... just as expected. Didn't you get my message?" I yelled.

Chalu stared at me, as though I was speaking a mixed dialect of Greek and Latin. He picked up his mobile and noticed my message that was left unopened along with at least ten other messages.

"Oh," he replied, with a ridiculous smirk and fixed his eyes back on the newspaper.

I went into the kitchen where Chalu's mother was at her operational best, exhibiting the art of multitasking.

"Hi, aunty, what's for breakfast?"

"I've made dosa. Take it from the table. Or if you can wait for some time, I will make some *paniyaram*."

"No no. We've no time. I'll have dosa," I said and walked to the dining table.

I was stunned to see Chalu still sitting on the couch, he hadn't moved an inch.

"Dai, we are getting late da. Go get ready," I yelled at him.

Chalu rubbed his stomach and showed me the victory sign, with the most disgusting expression on his face, indicating that he was still waiting for nature's call. I sighed at him in disbelief.

"Aunty, have you dropped the idea of making *paniyaram* yet?" I asked while surrendering myself to the transcendence of time as the hands of the clock pedalled past nine-forty.

• • •

The Honda Activa pleaded for mercy as I manoeuvred through buses, lorries, cars, auto rickshaws, bikes, cycles, pedestrians, dogs, speed breakers, bumps, humps, potholes, manholes, stones and everything else that came my way. Chalu sat behind me directing me through unimaginable gaps, overplaying the role of a personal traffic policeman. He even tried guiding fellow motorists through tiny cracks in between buses.

I looked at my watch. It was half past ten.

"God, we are late by an hour already. It's all because of you," I complained.

Chalu did not care about the accusation as he had his ears, eyes, nose, tongue and skin fixed on Poornima, his latest crush, who was also battling her way through the traffic. Going late to college wasn't new to us. There were instances when we got to college after lunchtime. There would be a problem every day. The alarm clock didn't go off, water scarcity, breakfast not ready, traffic, unwell, tyre puncture or forgot to wear pants were some of our most absurd excuses. But today, we had to reach on time. It was our investiture ceremony. I was to be badged the cultural secretary of the college, a proud designation I would accept and pile above other positions such as the Rotaract Club president, the college magazine editor and the college representative that I duly held.

"Hello, boys. Looks like your alarm clocks didn't go off today."

The voice sounded familiar to both Chalu and I. Our heads turned together in the direction of the voice. Mr. Illamparithi, the head of the visual communication department, smiled at us, seated on his sparkling black Pulsar.

Chalu jumped off the back of my Activa and landed in front of Illamparithi sir's bike.

"Sorry sir, as we suffered through a severe traffic jam and were unable to reach on time. I request you to grant us permission," he said, bowing humbly before Illamparithi sir.

Chalu generally did not flap his tongue brainlessly when he spoke to teachers. But Illamparithi sir was a cool customer. He was more of a friend to us than a teacher. He was an inspiring mentor and an extraordinary human being. He carried the pulse of the students and knew exactly where to draw lines of restrictions. His students respected him for his simplicity and flexibility.

"Don't worry boys. I guess at least half the people of the college are here," Illamparithi sir said.

"Why, sir?" I asked.

"A tree was uprooted in the rain last night. It has fallen right across the road."

"See! We would've been late even if we had started early," Chalu told me. "Everything happens for a reason. It was God who made your alarm clock go off at the wrong time, and it was the same God who kept me waiting for... you know what."

"Oh, then why did God make the others start early? And why would God go around fidgeting with everyone's alarm clock instead of just keeping the tree from falling?" I asked.

Chalu pretended not to have heard. He stood facing Illamparithi sir.

"Ummm... s-sir, shouldn't they have removed it early in the morning?" Chalu asked.

"I guess they were debating whether to cremate or bury it," Illamparithi sir joked.

"What do you think they would have decided sir?" Chalu asked.

"Do you care? Get on the bike. I guess they've cleared the tree. The traffic is moving," Illamparithi sir said.

Chalu got behind the Pulsar.

"Abi, see you in college," he said as Illamparithi sir rode forward.

"Get to the auditorium as soon as you get to college Abi. We're late already," Illamparithi sir said.

"Sure sir," I said and followed the Pulsar that sped away.

• • •

I rushed towards the auditorium fuming my way through familiar foes, who enthusiastically reminded me of my late arrival.

"Finally, the Shatabdi Express arrives," Nithin Menon teased.

"I'll deal with you after the ceremony," I yelled at him, as I ran into the auditorium.

There was complete silence in the auditorium except for the shrill screeches of the microphone.

"Damn!!! Looks like the guests have already come," I murmured to myself.

I hurried backstage, my mind browsing through dynamic pages of custom-made excuses. I tiptoed into the green room, slipped into my blazer and stepped out after making desperate attempts to adjust my unruly hair.

"What are you doing here?" Nithin asked. I was startled by the voice.

"Shhhhh..." I silenced him. "Don't let anyone know I am late. Thank God we decided to have the felicitation speeches in the beginning," I whispered.

"Excuse me. Didn't you take a look inside when you entered?" Nithin asked.

"N-no...," I said and peeked inside.

The stage was empty. The auditorium was unoccupied, except for a few sparrows that jumped from one seat to another, playing musical chairs. The sound controller was engaged in the tedious process of disconnecting and winding up the microphones. I was confused. I turned to Nithin, my heart pounding, my ears gathering up the courage to listen to the bad news.

"Over?" I asked, in a state of worry.

"No. Not yet. They've just decided to have the event post lunch."

"Why?" I asked, heaving a sigh of relief.

"There was a flight delay. The guests are stuck in the airport." Nithin said.

"How did you find out?"

"Sources...," Nithin replied, with a smile.

"Great. You will make a good journalist," I said, punching him in the stomach.

Nithin was also my classmate and a good friend. Apart from Nithin and Chalu, the fifteen others in my class transformed into good friends after being introduced to each other as mere classmates. Nithin always wanted to be the first person to be aware of news updates. He would go around the college eavesdropping on private conversations, hunting for latest information and gossip. It was he who dug out Chalu's inclination towards Poornima. Although he wore various tags such as the 'college news agent,' 'eavesdropper,' 'Sherlock Holmes,' 'All India Radio,' and 'Sleuthhound' he was good at keeping secrets.

He knew exactly what news to broadcast and what not to. Nithin wanted to be a successful journalist and knew quite well that he was walking steadily towards the direction of his dream.

My phone vibrated as I walked towards the classroom.

It was a text message from an unknown number.

Hey sweetheart. You're looking cute today.

I frowned as soon as I read the message. Nithin peered into my mobile.

Who is this? I texted back.

Your secret admirer...

I was convinced that someone was playing a prank. But, I secretly wished it wasn't a prank. After running through a slide show of possible suspects in my head, I decided to call and find out. I waited patiently as the phone rang, saving up all my anger to use up on the prankster.

The call was answered with a soft "hello" It was the voice of a young lady. My lips turned into a nervous smile. All the anger melted and leaked out through my forehead in the form of sweat.

"Who is this?" I asked, nervously.

"I told you. Your secret admirer," She replied.

I frowned, smiled and held my breath all at once. "Looks like you didn't shave today," She said before I could open my mouth to talk.

"Who are you?" I asked, my desperation reflecting in my tone.

"Turn to your right," She said.

I angled my neck to the right almost immediately. I noticed an attractive young girl with short hair, dressed in a baby pink *salwar-kameez*. I smiled, as I recognised who I was looking at.

"Jesse!!! You are so dead," I said, as I blushed and pounded towards her.

"Gotcha," Jesse shouted.

"You are so very mean. I almost fell for it."

"Almost fell? I saw you rolling on the floor as soon as you got my message. See! There is still some dust on your pants." She teased.

"Yeah, he refused to stand up even when I offered him help," Nithin said, adding more sugar to the coffee.

Jesse gave Nithin a high-five, as they realised that they had fixed their target for the day.

"UArrrggghhhh. I am going to kill you both," I said, holding Jesse's neck.

Jesse laughed. Nithin laughed even more, waking up his tickle nerves deliberately, making sure he mocked me as much as he could.

"I think I should change my number often. It's nice to see you at the receiving end." Jesse said.

"You can't trick me twice, girl," I said.

"Let's see. Why are you in a blazer? Do we have a fancy dress competition today?" Jesse asked.

"Bad joke," I said, giving her a thumbs down. "Don't tell me you didn't know we have our investiture ceremony today."

"Oh, yeah. I forgot. You actually look good in this blazer. But I guess you'll have to button your shirt completely," she said, pointing at the first button of my shirt that was left undone. "You've got to look formal, you know."

"Pah. I just hate it." I grunted. "Tucked in shirt. Choking neck ties. Polished shoes. Overheating blazers. I'd rather lie in a coffin."

"Tough luck, bro. I guess you'll have to start getting used to it. You will have to wear formals when you enter the corporate world," Jesse said.

"There's no way I am getting into a corporate. My professional life will begin and end on movie sets," I said.

Jesse glanced at me and smiled.

"You know, I have this vision that you will grow really big someday," Jesse said, with all her heart.

"Yeah, as big as a coconut tree that has all its nuts on its head," Nithin said and burst into laughter, raising his hand to give Jesse another high-five.

Jesse and I gave Nithin a disgusted look. Nithin stopped laughing and dropped his hand, after being turned down by Jesse.

"Y-you kn-now... a... tall... coconut... tree... with coconuts at the top. It's a joke." Nithin said, shrugging.

"Thoughtful... but pathetic." I said.

"Abi, why didn't you shave today?" Jesse asked.

"Ah, that's a long story," I replied with a sigh. "I'm planning to write a book someday. I'll make sure I include that episode in it."

"You look good with this tiny stubble though," Jesse said.

I blushed.

"Thanks. Now tell me. Are you looking for a favour from me? You have been blowing my trumpet from the time we met."

Jesse laughed.

"Actually, yes."

"What?"

"Where in the world is my darling boyfriend? I have been looking for him from the time I got to college."

"Nithin is in charge of the lost and found department," I said, pointing at Nithin.

"Ummm... I saw him last in our television production studio. He was allegedly found molesting a junior girl, trying to get her to express emotions that she could hardly imagine" Nithin said.

"Can you do me a favour when you get there?" Jesse asked. "Can you flush his mobile phone down the closet? That fat ass has not answered one call."

"I guess you can do that yourself. Students from other departments are allowed in the studio today. We're conducting some kind of a talk show," Nithin said.

"Can we go now?" Jesse asked.

"Why not? As long as you promise me you'll kick his centre in front of those junior girls. Every one of them is behind him," Nithin said, with a pinch of jealousy hidden in his voice.

"That's right. He is in the studio 24×7, and all the girls make sure they stay with him so that they can skip their theory classes," I said.

Jesse's ears turned into a chimney as she fumed. Nithin signalled to me to keep the stove turned on. She unzipped her bag and took out her chef knife.

"Take me there right now. I'm going to kill him," she said, blowing away a strand of hair that fell on her face.

Jesse was a hotel management student in the same college. She was more like a sister to me than a friend. She was rich, beautiful and kind-hearted. But no one dared to exploit her credits as she was the daughter of a local MLA. She fell in love with Renjith when they were in the first year simply because she liked the way he asked her out. He apparently pleaded with her to take part in a play that he was directing, in which she had to play a poet who proposes to her lover through her poems. After the play, he expressed his love for her using the verses of the same poem in front of a crowd of close friends. Poor Jesse found herself melting in love, completely unaware of the fact that Renjith had stolen the proposal idea from an old Malayalam movie. Jesse's world had revolved around Renjith ever since and vice versa.

• • •

2

Renjith's House in Coimbatore

I stood staring at the clock as memories rushed through my head making me feel dizzy. I placed the clock back in the showcase and glanced outside the window, my fingers making circles in my thick beard.

"How many times did we speak after you eloped?" I asked Renjith, who sat at the dining table with Jesse on his lap.

He had one arm around her, and the other was on the dining table, holding his quota of whisky.

"A few times," Renjith said, taking some time to recollect the exact number and ultimately failing.

"That's how life is. Isn't it? Work and family turn out to be our priorities. We forget to keep in touch," I said.

"Abi, I didn't mean to..."

"It's okay." I interrupted. "I am not blaming you. I am not blaming anybody. I could have kept in touch too. But I didn't either."

"What about the others?" Renjith asked.

"They're all scattered. I haven't been in touch with anybody for years until I met Peri and Chalu yesterday."

I looked out of the window again. "The real world is different, Renji. It's full of hate, ego, greed, competition and betrayal."

I gulped down my whisky in one go and squawked. "Can you pour me one more?"

Renjith took the bottle of Jack Daniels and placed it on the table.

"Help yourself."

I walked up to the table and helped myself to a double large. I dragged the chair, making it screech and sat down to face Renjith and Jesse eye to eye.

"Tell me your story," I said. "When did you move to Coimbatore?"

"A year after we got married," Renjith replied. "We left for Kerala a few days after our wedding. Her folks accepted us after a year of trying. Now we're here. Living separately. This is her dad's house."

I looked around surveying the well-kept house. There were books and movie CDs arranged neatly in a glass shelf. A little fish tank with a few gold fish stood in the corner of the room. I noticed a few framed photographs of his and Jesse's family on the top shelf. Amid them was an old picture of us in college; eighteen of us had clicked it when we were in the second year.

"Impressive," I said. "Looks like you've been doing a lot of reading."

"Yes. Reference for a little script work I am doing."

"Are you writing a script?"

"Well, I haven't locked in on a story yet. But I am definitely looking for one. My dad-in-law has finally accepted to produce my movie. But he has to like my script."

"Whoa. That's awesome," I said, my eyes widening in excitement.

"Not as great as you think. It's been a couple of years since he gave me this offer. I have told him four stories already. He isn't impressed yet."

"Quite a hard nut to crack, huh?" I asked. Renjith smiled.

"But I can't believe a hard nut like him managed to produce a soft nut like Jesse," Renjith said, holding her tighter.

Jesse slapped him playfully. I laughed.

"You guys have always made a great pair," I said. "The last time I met you guys was on the day you eloped. Jesse, you look absolutely the same, but your Renji has gained a few kilos. I can't believe it's been eight years since we met."

I sighed and leaned back in my chair as the whisky slowly started creating waves in my brain.

"Now will you tell us what happened to you?" Renjith demanded softly.

I leaned forward, picked my glass up and looked into the eyes of my interrogators, who appeared to be very keen on getting an answer. It was four powerful eyes versus two dilated ones. I had to surrender.

"Okay," I said.

• • •

3

Chalu's Outburst

"Emotion. Emotion. I need more emotion, Aruna," Renjith said, as he ran his fingers through his thick, long, curly hair and guided it towards the back of his head. "Aarthi, do you have a hair band?" He asked, turning to a thin, cute girl, who looked like a live version of a Barbie doll.

"Phew, this hair is taking half my life out," he said.

"Why don't you cut it, *anna*?" Aarthi asked as she gave Renjith a hair band.

"No way. Not until we stage this play successfully," Renjith said and tied his overgrown hair into an untidy ponytail. "So Aruna, where were we?"

"Oh dear Prince, our love will blossom at the far end of the horizon and will descend deep into the sea," Aruna said, her hands and face moving by default, as she lost count of the number of times she had rehearsed the same portion.

"Renju, you haven't explained Aruna's character to us yet," Deepika said.

"Aruna is playing a poet who falls in love with a prince and expresses her love for him through her poems."

"Woooooowwww." The girls whooped making it look like Aruna had just been roped into James Cameron's next movie.

"Interesting. But don't you think it is a little old?" I asked, standing on the threshold of the studio, removing my blazer as though I was preparing for some action.

"A couple of years old to be precise," Nithin added.

"Oh, guys. W-When d-did you g-get here. Ummm... I-it's not that stupid old amateur play that we did in the first year," Renjith said, surprised by our unanticipated entry.

"It was a stupid old amateur play YOU did," Nithin said, correcting him.

"Yeah, whatever. It's not that. It's the story of another poet who falls in love with another prince. You know, with different names and all. I am going to introduce Aruna this time. She will do the lead role."

"Oh wow. Sounds convincing," I said. "Speaking of introductions, we would like to introduce to you a very special person."

"Who is it?" Renjith asked, his eyes widening in excitement.

"Ladies and GENTLEMAN, I take this great opportunity to introduce to you JESSE!!!"

Nithin and I made way for Jesse as she ran into the studio with a knife in her hand.

"Renjith. I am going to kill you." She shouted as she ran.

"Oh. Jess... eee... You-u...? Ho-ow-w...? I... What?"

The words just did not come out. Renjith realised that he had no time to talk. He had to run.

"How many times do I have to call you? Monkey, moron, idiot...," she shouted as she charged towards him.

"Jesse... I f-forgot to... I mean... I was busy." He shouted back, as he ran all over the place evading her attacks.

Renjith jumped over a table, rolled on the floor, tripped over a wire and rammed against the wall before he made an exit with Jesse following close behind him.

I gave Nithin a high-five as we laughed uncontrollably, enjoying every bit of the scene.

"Now what are you girls doing here? Go to your classes." Nithin roared, scaring the girls.

The girls picked their bags and scurried out of the studio without saying a word.

"Fantastic. This is what you would call a perfect eviction plan," Nithin declared, dusting his palms.

"You bet," I admitted.

"Okay. Our work here is over. What next?" Nithin asked.

"Don't we have classes?"

"No, da. We don't have classes today. We are supposed to be preparing for the talk show."

"Talk show? When was this planned?" I asked.

"Ah, don't bother. Peri and Bala will take care of it." Nithin said.

"Alright, you want to have some tea?" I asked.

"Oh, I will need gallons. Let's go."

"Okay. Turn off the lights and air-conditioners. I'll fetch the key."

We headed towards the canteen, our hearts filled with contentment as we knew our beloved friend wouldn't dare look into the face of any other girl, at least for the next couple of weeks.

• • •

"Amala *chechi*!!! Two cups of tea," I shouted as I entered the canteen.

Amala *chechi* was the canteen supervisor. She was a kind-hearted yet short-tempered lady from Kerala, who settled down in Chennai when her favourite Tamil actor, MGR, was elected as the Chief Minister of Tamil Nadu. Even after being tormented in chaotic queues for metro water and ration and associating with Tamil people for over two decades, she hadn't managed to get rid of the Malayalam accent in her Tamil. People could visualise a heterogeneous collage of Kathakali, boat races, *sadhya*, Kalari fights and Onam celebrations orbiting around her whenever she opened her mouth to speak. It was this adherent accent that earned her the adherent surname '*chechi*'.

The food in Amala *chechi's* canteen was always special as she carefully mixed secret ingredients of love, care and bits of advice too, at times, before she served them. She took the liberty of advising or scolding anyone as she considered the students her own children.

"Ah!!! There you are. I was just wondering why you hadn't come yet. Don't you children attend classes?" Amala *chechi* grumbled.

"Oh *chechi*, how can we sit in class when the mouthwatering aroma of your *bhajji* is all over the place?" I teased.

"If it is the smell of *bhajji* that brought you here, why don't you buy some along with your tea?" *chechi* asked, as she placed two cups of tea on the counter.

"There's a reason behind that," I said.

"What?"

"Your *bhajjis* smell nice. But they don't taste good." I said, jokingly.

"What about the tea?" Nithin asked, pretending to be serious.

"Oh, the tea tastes delicious. But don't you dare smell it. Hold your nose and gulp it down," I said, chuckling.

"Get lost, before I break your heads," Amala *chechi* screamed, picking up a hot *tava* from the stove and holding it upright.

Nithin and I dispersed in two different directions with our cups of tea while laughing. We seated ourselves in our favourite location, by the canteen window, from where we could see a variety of pretty girls from other departments sitting on stone benches with their eyes glued to their books. As we made ourselves comfortable, Nithin noticed something that made him smile.

"Look at that," he said, pointing at a table behind us.

I turned back and noticed Renjith and Jesse seated facing each other, completely lost in a world of love, totally oblivious to what was happening around them.

"How sweet. I hope they don't go beyond just looking at each other," I joked, turning away and facing Nithin.

"There you are. Caught you at last!" Peri exclaimed as though he had just spotted an inmate who had escaped from his custody.

He frisbeed a half-used roll of cellophane tape towards me as he walked in, followed by Bala. The cellophane tape lost elevation much before it reached me and disappeared into Renjith's thick hair.

Perinbanathan Kathiresan and Balasaravanan Soundarajan, one named after the length of the Cheran Express and the other after the Howrah Express, were also a part of the viscom family. Their respective trains were reduced to the sizes of their engines, when they learned that their friends found it difficult to travel from one end to the other, thus cutting short their names to Peri and Bala.

Peri was an upcoming graphic and web designer, whose exceptional designs had already won laurels in various competitions at the national level.

Bala was a sincere lover boy. He would fall in deep, passionate love with a random girl in the college until he realised that she was not interested in him. He would then switch his focus to another random girl, falling in deep, passionate love with her.

"Have you finished preparing for the talk show?" Nithin asked Peri.

"Almost done. I finished preparing the set. Have to install it in the studio."

"Abi, do you want to host today's show?" Bala asked.

"I don't mind. How are you paying me? Cheque or cash?" I teased.

"Huh? You'll have to pay us for letting you host the show," Bala replied.

"Okay, I don't have any cash right now. How about some *bhajji* instead?"

"Yeah. Fair enough."

"Then go get us four plates of *bhajji.*"

Peri quickly grabbed the chair next to me and sat down before Bala could pass the order to him.

"Go, Bala. Go. Four plates of *bhajji* with little coconut chutney," Peri repeated the order.

"Dog. You go get it," Bala said.

"Bala. Do some work once in a while for God's sake. You know, I made the entire set myself. He just sat there messaging his new found girl," Peri said as he removed a few sticky ropes of Fevicol that was stuck to his hand.

"Okay okay. Stop complaining. Abi, you come with me. You have to pay anyway." Bala said.

"Just go *da*. I'll pay her later. Tell her I asked for it," I said and winked at Nithin, reminding him of the feedback we had given *chechi* a while ago.

"All you guys are hopeless," Bala hissed and stormed away towards the counter.

"*Chechi*, four plates of bhajji for Abi," he shouted as he walked.

Nithin, Peri and I turned our heads towards the counter as we heard the sound of a crash followed by a few heavily-built words. Bala returned with chutney on his face.

"What on earth did you say to her? She slammed the vessel of chutney on the counter, and it just splashed on my face."

"Oh, I just gave her some negative feedback. I guess this is how she responds to it," I chuckled.

Nithin and Peri burst into laughter.

"Shut up you idiots," Bala snapped. "GO. Go get the *bhajjis.*"

"Okay. Okay. I'm going," I said and darted towards the counter.

I returned with the plates of *bhajji* after using a bucket of oiled, greased and buttered words that fought tolerantly through an array of high-pitched, big-muscled blasts.

"Do you want to sit here?" I asked as I placed the plates of *bhajji* on the table. "Shall we go to the stone bench?"

"Okay. Let's go," the others replied and we headed towards our favourite location.

• • •

Beyond the neatly mowed college football court, far away from the hubbub that echoed from the building walls, under the placidity of a yellow flame tree, blanketed by tender buds of fresh yellow flowers, was a little stone bench. This stone bench was the pastime headquarters of the students of the visual communication department. The place, after being discovered by Harish, another dear member of the visual communication clan, when we were in the second year, was where we spent the careless hours of our jobless days, chatting away the long pages of our life history.

We arrived at the stone bench with the plates of *bhajjis* in our hands.

"Ah, this is life." I sighed as I sat on the stone bench after pushing a bed of flowers off it.

"Yeah. You bet. I'm going to miss this place after college," Peri said, nibbling on the edges of a *bhajji*.

My eyes wandered through the football court as my mind dissolved into a stream of memories that channelled themselves into an ocean of thoughts about my translucent future. Everyone remained silent all of a sudden. The very thought of having to leave college paralysed our hearts. Each one of us had our own dream and was excited about getting to it as fast as we possibly could. But, starting a career with an entirely new set of people, far away from college and friends, was something we hadn't really thought of. Life has to be lived in phases. That is how it is designed. We were not the first ones in this situation. But we were facing this situation for the first time.

"Guys!" Harish shouted as he came in running. "Get to the department as soon as possible," he said, gasping for breath.

"What's the matter?" Peri queried.

"Chalu is off his head. He's ripping off all his paintings that he had put on the department walls."

"What the f-ff... what's wrong with him?" I snarled. "I don't know. We'd better get there before he rips the department apart," Harish warned.

• • •

My Humble Lady, a beautiful portrait that emoted mixed expressions of happiness, sorrow, anger, domination and submission of a young lady, welcomed us with a big hole on her nose. Peri and I looked at each other, thoroughly shocked by the disfigured face of the painting as we knew the effort Chalu had taken to add life to it. We rushed upstairs and found him removing all his paintings that decorated the department walls.

"What the fuck is wrong with you?" I barked, as I charged towards him.

"Abi, this is none of your business. I know what I am doing," Chalu shouted back.

"Will you bloody tell us what happened here?" Peri hollered.

Illamparithi sir, Suresh sir, Arun sir, Bibu Sir, Ramesh Sir and Gandhimathi ma'am rushed to the spot after being informed about the issue. Chalu broke down as soon he saw them. Tears rolled down his cheeks instantly.

"You all know how much that painting in the department entrance means to me," he said, his voice breaking.

"Which one? My humble lady?" Peri asked.

"Yes... Some son of a b...tore it," he said, controlling his language in front of his teachers. "I don't trust anyone anymore. I am taking all my paintings home. My paintings are my life. I put my soul into every painting of mine. I don't want to put them at risk. I..."

"Chalu, this is not the way you react to this." Illamparithi sir intervened. "You could have spoken to us. What are we here for?"

"Sir, I know exactly what I am doing," Chalu said.

"Boy, control your tongue. You are talking to your HOD," Suresh sir warned him.

Chalu remained silent. "I am sorry sir," he said.

"I understand your situation, Chalu. We know how much your work means to you. We love your work too. I'll make sure I find the person who did it. We are always here to help you out. I have no right to restrict you from taking your paintings home. But remember your paintings are our pride. Every visitor who walks into our department is awestruck by your work. I don't think it would be good if they knew the creator of so much awe is weak in character. Do not make such impulsive decisions. Small issues like this can spoil the reputation you've built over the years. The world outside is not going to be a walk in the park. You will be washed, battered, wrung and put out to dry. It is the character in you that will help you withstand stressful situations. Try to master the art of controlling your emotions. You all have a long way to go, children."

Illamparithi sir's words were so inspiring. Life was all about understanding people. He knew exactly how Chalu felt and his mature reaction to the situation eased his temper.

"I am really sorry sir. I will put these paintings back on the walls," Chalu assured.

"Good. I am glad you understand," he said. We stepped forward to help him.

"Does anyone have a cellophane tape?" Chalu asked.

Peri dug his hand into Renjith's thick hair and pulled out the roll of cellophane tape that he lost in the canteen.

"Where did that come from?" Renjith asked dumbstruck.

"This is called Jesse magic," Peri said.

Everyone, except Renjith, burst into laughter.

• • •

"There! This looks exactly like your dad's head now. Bald in the centre and small patches of hair on both sides," Peri told me, as he ripped out the fluffy green portion from the center part of a tennis ball.

I laughed.

"Dog! This is how you will look in the future," I said, placing my almost worn-out bat against the waist-high wall of Chalu's multi purpose terrace.

Chalu's terrace was one of our most common meeting places outside college. Unlike other terraces that were used only by maids to put washed clothes to dry, Chalu's terrace had multiple purposes.

It was used as an assembling point after our outings and for our get-togethers. Chalu used it for his occasional yoga, meditation, workout and martial arts training sessions. However, the sessions were practiced seasonally depending on his mood and the type of movies he watched.

When he watched a Jackie Chan movie, he would be found undergoing rigorous martial arts training, which would last for not more than a couple of days as he would have watched a spiritual movie the third day and consequently switched to yoga and meditation. The terrace was also used as a cricket pitch, mostly when Nithin, Peri and I, the only cricket lovers in our circle, were around.

Chalu also used the terrace for painting experiments, sometimes using his palms and feet as paintbrushes. He had once even gone to the extent of dipping himself in paint and rolling all over the canvas, naming it the 'body brush act.' We had to use a laundry brush to remove the paint from his body later on. Apart from all these, the terrace was also used for booze parties, dance and play rehearsals, rain water harvesting, thanks to the government, and of course to dry clothes, which was a default process in the 'usage of terrace' rulebook.

"Today was a very eventful day, wasn't it?" Peri said.

"Yes. The road block, the eviction plan, the *bhajji* episode and the investiture ceremony," I said, listing the day's events as I summarized them.

"You forgot Chalu's outburst," Peri said, contributing his share to the events listing.

Chalu turned away from us and faced the neighbour's terrace. Angelynn, his eighteen-year-old neighbour, walked to and fro along the length of the terrace with a book titled, 'Fiscal Economics'.

Studying! This was something that Chalu's multi purpose terrace did not witness since the time the building had been constructed.

"You really love her, don't you?" I asked.

"*Chee*, no way. She is just a potential sight piece," Chalu said.

"I am talking about Poornima. Are you serious about her?"

Chalu remained silent for a moment. Peri and I exchanged quick glances.

"Yaaah, *da*," he said, his voice cracking.

He sniffed and turned to his friends. The street lights glimmered in his eyes as the tears threatened to roll down his cheeks.

"You spoke to her today, didn't you?" Peri asked.

"Yaaah, *da*," he said.

"Did you ask her out?" I asked.

"Yaaah, *da*." His tone perfectly matched his previous *yaaah da*.

"And, she turned you down?" I asked, making sure I polished my modulation to make it less hurtful.

Chalu replied with another identical *yaaah da.*

"What did she say?" Peri asked.

"She said she came here to study."

"That's all?"

"No. She said I was over-ambitious by thinking I could impress her just because the college believes I am an artist."

"Clear fucking attitude, *macha.* How can she!" Peri fumed.

I gestured for him to stay silent for a moment.

"And so you vented your anger on *My Humble Lady*?"

There was a moment of silence. Chalu fixed his eyes back on Angelynn. Was it because his potential sight piece looked hot today or was it because he couldn't face his friends, who had just found him guilty?

"Yaaah, da." His voice played its favourite tone of the day again.

Peri and I exchanged 'see-I-told-you' looks.

"You guys know very well that My Humble Lady was an abstract portrait of her. I love her so much *da.* I just couldn't accept the rejection. I was angry, upset and frustrated."

"But why did you remove your other paintings?" Peri asked.

He was genuinely confused.

"I just didn't know what to do. It took me some time to realise that I had destroyed my favourite painting. What would I say if anyone asked? I had to create a scene to cover my mistake. Illamparithi sir was right. I reacted impulsively, but *My Humble Lady* was the victim of my impulsive act. The so-called 'Chalu's outburst' was a complete drama."

Peri and I looked at each other like we had just solved a crossword puzzle. We had gotten the answers to all our questions. Chalu looked relieved. He was not the type who could keep secrets for long. He would have spilled the beans even if we had not interrogated him.

"Now, coming to the comment she made about your passion. She is going to pay for that." Peri huffed.

"Shut up! I have forgiven her for that. After all, that's what God says. Forgive and forget," Chalu said.

"I think even God was in love with someone when he made that statement," Peri said.

"Yeah. He loves all of us."

"Man. I love this girl. She is hot," I said, ignoring the discussion and staring at Angelynn.

Chalu and Peri realised that they had better things to do than debate about who God loved. They turned and fixed their looks on her. Suddenly, the lights went off. Angelynn shut her fiscal economics and ran downstairs squealing in the darkness.

"Damn! These power cuts are a curse to poor students like...," I stopped midway.

"Students like?" Chalu and Peri asked in chorus.

"Students like us."

The poor students in us burst out laughing.

• • •

4

A Golden Opportunity

College life was over. My friends dissipated into different directions in an attempt to chase their respective dreams. Some were placed in reputed companies through campus recruitment. Some went on to pursue higher education. I did not want to go for higher studies. I wanted to focus on my dream of turning into a reputed actor. The serial in which I was acting was dropped due to a few issues at the production house. I spent an entire year waiting for its release, simultaneously hoping I would hear from Shruthi.

Her number was not in use anymore. She had moved from her house in Anna Nagar. I sent her dozens of emails, which possibly sat in her inbox unopened. There was absolutely no way to reach her. She had vanished from my life, leaving me no hope of a reunion. Although I wasn't completely over her, I began to get used to the pain of living without her.

I had to. Because family responsibilities slowly started creeping up my shoulders. My dad fell ill and retired from his business. I slowly started turning into the 'go-to' man when it came to paying bills and other expenses. My only relief in my career over the past year was that a short film, which I had directed back in college, had won the best film award at an international short film festival. I had won five thousand dollars, which helped me a great deal to cover the expenses of my father's illness and other requirements at home. Otherwise, it was hard times altogether. I had sent my portfolio to various production houses around Chennai in vain. All I was left with was about half a lakh rupees in my bank account and a few months time to cement my career in films.

Just as I began to lose hope, I received a call from a person named Jairam. He introduced himself as the manager of an upcoming Tamil film, and he told me that he found my profile on some website, where I had posted my pictures on some random desperate day. Jairam invited me to an audition and photo shoot in Gobichettipalayam, Tamil Nadu, whispering to me inside information that I was already selected and that the audition was just going to be a formality.

I suddenly felt I was infused with hydrogen gas that made me ascend high. However, Jairam had a small catch that could have probably reduced the level of hydrogen gas in me a little.

"Abhishek, since this is just a test shoot, you will have to bear the expenses of the costume and make-up." he said.

"How much?" I asked, praying from within that he didn't ask for an amount that I wouldn't be able to afford.

"Ten thousand," he said.

My mind quickly accessed my bank account balance. I started making rough calculations in my head.

"Don't worry Abhishek, the money will be refunded along with your remuneration when the movie commences," he said, responding to my silence.

"Okay," I said.

I did not worry about it much, as it was just one-fifth of the total money I had and did not mind spending it, considering the golden opportunity I would get in return.

Moreover, I was going to get it back along with my pay. It sounded like a fair deal to me.

The same time the next day, I was at Gobichettipalayam all set to do something that I had been yearning to do for years. I called Jairam to request him to send the pick-up taxi that he had promised he would send. Jairam, however, told me that there were issues with the pick-up and requested me to take a bus to Sathyamangalam. after making sure he apologised for the inconvenience caused. When I reached Sathyamangalam, I learned from him that some taxi strike had cropped up during my two-hour journey from Gobichettipalayam, which I felt, was a figment of his imagination as I saw at least 263 taxis around me. Another apology landed me in a bus that was heading to Kadambur, a hill station near Sathyamangalam. However, I fell into a little puddle of suspicion.

Finally, by the end of the day, I managed to meet him, the director Suresh Lal and the producer Vishwa Mohan, who appeared to be really excited to meet me. I wasn't too sure if it was my portfolio or the money I carried that excited them.

"Ah. Abhishek. You are finally here," director Suresh Lal said. "I am extremely sorry for giving you the trouble of travelling here all by yourself. There was a miscommunication. Our driver thought there was a taxi strike today and did not turn up."

"No problem, sir," I said.

This reduced my suspicion. I realized that the production manager communicated a different story to me. Maybe they were genuine people wanting to make a good movie.

"We watched your short film, *Uravu*, online. Your performance was amazing," the producer said.

"Yes, I cast you in my mind the moment I saw the movie. All this audition and make-up test is just going to be a formality," said Suresh Lal.

"Wait and watch. You will have a bright life post the release of this movie. I assure you that," the producer said.

I was thrilled and relieved that I was on the threshold of success. As committed, the audition and photo shoot happened the next day after Jairam made sure I gave him the ten thousand rupees they had asked for.

Suresh Lal was overwhelmed by my performance in the audition.

"You are a perfect fit for the character," he said, patting my back.

"I am pleased to hear that," I said.

"Okay buddy, listen. This is the role of a second lead. I want you to grow a beard and lose some weight."

A year of joblessness had encouraged some flab to build a circle around my waist.

"When are we shooting sir?" I asked, eager to know how much time I had to reduce my weight.

"In a couple of months. We are attending to some logistic issues now. We will start rolling by September."

Two months was more than sufficient to burn the fat and grow some facial hair. I suddenly felt relieved and exuberant that everything went smoothly.

• • •

Back at home, I counted every growing inch of my beard as much as I counted down every gram I exuviated each passing day. I looked at myself in the mirror exactly 42 days later and realised that I had lost about four kilos. The smile that hid under my thick beard grew wider and more palpable when I received a call from Vishwa Mohan, the producer.

"Abhishek, I have some bad news and good news for you," he said.

"What is it, sir?" I asked, hoping the good news was great and the bad news was negligible.

"Well, the bad news is – the actor, who was supposed to be playing the lead in our movie, met with an accident and broke his hand."

"Oh! I am sorry. I hope he is recovering well," I said.

"He is. But the people here are high on sentiments. He feels that this is a bad phase for him and is not an appropriate time to do a movie. He offered to co-produce the movie, and now I am beginning to consider dropping the entire project."

I was alarmed. I did not know if I had the strength to face a drop. I was reminded of the good news that he had in his kitty.

"Sir, what's the good news?" I asked, not wanting to respond to his idea of dropping the film.

"I have convinced the director to make you play the main lead. I know you have the potential."

I felt someone lifting me high up in the air.

"If you can co-produce the movie, you can play the lead," he said.

I was dropped from mid-air. I fell to the floor with a thud.

"Sir, I do not have the capacity to do that," I said.

"Then I am afraid we will have to part ways, Abhishek. I am going to drop the project. I shall let you know if things work out. But please think it over. It is an opportunity of a lifetime." He hung up.

I did not even have the strength to think about it. I realised this was yet another ray of hope that just got stabbed in the back. Why was it so difficult to find a way into movies? Was cinema only meant for the people who had money? Did I have to get used to back to back failures?

I glanced at my mirror. I could feel my beard laughing in triumph as it could finally come off my cheeks. Was the producer actually making a movie or was this all a set-up to snatch a few bucks? There were quite a few people who took part in the audition, and he would have easily lapped up at least a hundred thousand rupees. I was confused and upset. I couldn't believe that such people existed in cinema. I was being exposed to the truth the hard way.

It is inhumanely cheap to exploit someone's dream for your gain.

I did nothing but stare at myself in the mirror. I felt like a clown, whose pants were pulled down when attempting to do a circus trick. Tears moistened my eyes.

I really wished Shruthi was with me that moment. She was the only person who could instil some encouragement in me. I wanted to hold her hand and rest on her lap. I wanted her to caress my hair, kiss my forehead and tell me that things would get better. I missed her terribly.

• • •

5

College Culturals and the Wizguys

Angelynn, I love you. Truly, madly and deeply. I am crazy about you. I want you to be in my life forever. Please don't leave me Angelynn," I said, standing in front of my mirror with tears in my eyes.

I quickly turned to my sister, who had her earphones plugged in. She was reading a book, gently tapping her feet to the music she was listening to.

"How was it?" I asked, unaware of the fact that she hadn't been looking at my performance.

"How was what?" She asked, removing her earphones.

"My acting..."

Veena rolled her eyes. It took her a moment to realise that I had been performing in front of the mirror.

"Oh! It was fantastic," she lied, fearing I would repeat my performance in case I knew she wasn't watching.

"Thank you. I've got one more variety. Watch."

I turned towards the mirror again. Veena plugged her earphones back and increased the volume.

"Angelynn..." I started again.

Just then my phone buzzed. I looked at my mobile screen. It was Ilamparithi sir. Veena used the opportunity to walk out of the room before falling victim to my acting practice.

"Hello, Abi. Good time to talk?" Ilamparithi sir asked.

"Yes sir."

"Do we have a music band?" he asked.

"No sir."

"Do you think we can start one?"

"We can try. But why, sir?" I asked.

"MCC has invited us for culturals. I am working on the participants' list to get your bonafides. I was just wondering if we could take part in light music too."

"Our music team is inexperienced. But we can still try," I said.

"Alright. We'll talk about it tomorrow. Sorry for calling at this time. I just got a little excited," he said.

"No problem at all, sir. Take care. Goodnight."

"Goodnight, Abi," he said and hung up.

I glanced at the mirror again.

"Angelynn, I am very sorry, Angelynn. My HOD called," I began.

• • •

"Will you stop spraying your spit into my flute?" Sreedev said, snatching his flute from me.

"Why isn't there any sound when I blow into it?" I asked.

"That needs practice," Sreedev replied.

We were preparing for our first cultural event of the year, which was to be conducted by the Madras Christian College.

We were setting up our first ever music band. The department was just three years old then, and there were hardly any musicians around. But Ilamparithi sir and I decided to try our luck.

"Are you sure we should do this, Abi?" Illamparithi sir asked, after listening to the first round of practice.

"I'm pretty sure, sir. We are good at all the other events. We've never participated in light music for the past two years. It's okay if we don't win. I want to make sure we participate."

"Okay. I leave it to you. Make sure you bring the overall trophy."

"We'll do our best, sir," I said and turned to my friends.

"Alright. Let's have another round of practice guys. Just a few quick suggestions. Vivek, I guess you should try singing rather than screaming. Sreedev, you're doing well. although I can't understand what a flute is doing in this song. Gautham, you should stop imitating Dave Mustaine and concentrate on playing the right chords. And Chalu, stop dancing around and get the fuck out of here."

Chalu raised his middle finger.

"Okay, guys let's do it again," I shouted, not bothering to even look at Chalu.

Chalu started dancing again and stopped as soon as the song was over. I folded my arms across my chest.

"I don't think this is getting anywhere, guys," I said. "It's not our fault. We are just beginners. But it's okay, let's just do it."

• • •

The Madras Christian College was in 'loud' mode with maximum volume. The cultural event was conducted exclusively for media students across Chennai. The Viscom troop of the Masan Memorial College stepped in.

I took a deep breath. We had won the overall trophy the previous year and were keen on repeating history. Renjith bent down and touched the floor before entering the campus.

"Don't you think you are overdoing your role?" Nithin asked.

"You will never understand my sentiments," Renjith said.

"Thank God. I don't want to."

"WIZGUYS!!!! TONIGHT WE DINE IN HELL!!!" Renjith suddenly screamed.

His voice was so strong that the area around froze for a moment. The trees stopped swaying. The crows were stuck in mid-air. The dogs appeared so shocked that they couldn't even bark. The people around had their eyes glued to him, looking baffled.

Renjith realised that his sentiments were getting too violent. He glanced at the people around him and simpered.

"I-I was actually practising for our play," he said.

The trees, the crows, the dogs and the people heaved a sigh of relief and continued with what they were doing. Renjith looked around to find us still staring at him.

"Shit happens," he said shrugging.

"True. However, I did not understand the WIZGUYS part," Nithin said.

"That's our new team name. I am not going to ask if you people like it. Like it or not, this is going to be our team name."

The Wizguys held their heads.

"Let's go, guys," I said.

The entire college was decorated with blue and white balloons. There were huge banners of the events and their sponsors all over the place. A variety of food counters were lined up right from the entrance up till the auditorium. The place was noisy. The air was filled with the smell of a mixed variety of food. The area looked beautiful. On the whole, it was a treat to the eyes, ears, nose and the tongue too for those who tasted the food.

As we walked in, we could hear the faint whispers of other college students.

"Hey, look. That's the Masan Memorial College. They won the overall trophy last year. They're good. I liked their play, it was hilarious."

The whispers were all over the place.

"Nithin, what's the first event?" I asked.

Nithin said something, but his voice was overlapped by the loud screech of a mike, followed by a very unpleasant female voice.

"Participants, who have not registered for the light music event, please do as soon as possible, as the event is going to begin in ten minutes."

Nithin shrugged. I glanced at my watch and scurried to the registration counter. On my way, I noticed participants practising their throats out.

"Damn, we've not even had one final rehearsal today," I told myself.

I quickly registered our team and walked back to my friends.

"Okay, guys. Shall we have one final rehearsal?"

"That's not needed, *macha*. I guess we are spot on." Gautham replied.

The mike screeched again. An unpleasant female voice followed.

"Alright, we are about to begin the light music event. Let me just run you all through the rules. You will be given fifteen minutes on stage. Three minutes for arranging your instruments and tuning up and twelve minutes to perform. You will have to sing two songs and give us one instrumental solo performance."

My eyes widened. I glared at Nithin.

"Fifteen minutes??? I thought you told me six minutes."

Nithin checked the rules brochure. He looked up at me and simpered.

"I'm sorry, *macha*, I read you out the rules of street play."

"What the fuck?" I snatched the brochure from him and took a glance.

I glared at Nithin again.

"Oh God! We're so screwed."

"That's okay *da*. We can always back off. They've mentioned it in the rules." Nithin said.

"Shut up. We are not backing off. Wait let me think."

I held my head. Nithin turned towards the food counter.

"Is anyone hungry, guys?" he asked, as though he had just spotted a food joint at a picnic spot and started to walk towards the pastries that had the word 'eat me' written all over them.

I held him by the collar of his shirt. "Not yet." I pulled him back. "Okay, guys. Listen. Here's the plan."

We made the team huddle just like the Indian cricket team would do before a match. A few guys threw in some comments as they passed by.

"Look at that. Team Masan Memorial is all set to rock."

Meanwhile, inside the huddle, I had begun to explain my master plan.

"Guys, we might not win this. But, let's not appear unprepared. They're going to give us fifteen minutes. It would be embarrassing if we finish it off in six minutes. But we've practised only one song. We have three minutes for tuning and setting up our instruments right?"

Everybody nodded their heads in unison.

"Well, we've got to waste some more time on that. Let's take six minutes. Pretend that you are not happy with the sound and keep working on it for six minutes."

Everybody scratched their heads in unison.

"Now we've got nine minutes. Let's take five minutes for our song. How many minutes do we have left?"

"Four!" The answer came in unison.

"Right. Ananth, you are good on the drums. Please, please do an instrumental solo for us. I am sure you can create some impromptu music for a good four minutes."

Ananth took a moment to make up his mind.

"Right. I'll do it."

"Cool. So as soon as Ananth finishes his instrumental solo, the timer will go off. And then we'll pretend that we are upset we could not sing our second song."

Nithin looked at me with disgust.

"That's cheap."

"Cheap, indeed. And if the plan is messed up, you are dead sheep."

"I request one representative from each team to come down to the registration table and pick up your lot for the light music event."

It was a different voice this time. It was sweet even after it fought through the annoying shrieks. My heart pounded as soon as I heard the announcement.

"It's about time, guys."

• • •

I waited patiently as the other college participants tugged and shoved around the registration counter as though someone was offering them free *jalebis*.

The crowd slowly dissipated revealing a cute girl, standing with outstretched hands that held a bowl. I stepped forward and looked into it. The bowl was wrapped inside five beautiful fingers that had neatly painted nails. There was just one chit inside the bowl.

"That's the only one left." The girl holding the bowl said.

She had a cute accent.

"I guess that's self-explanatory," I said.

She smiled. She had an attractive dimple. Her red nail polish matched perfectly with her red kurti. She wore just the right amount of *kajal* to make her eyes look like a dream.

I quickly picked up the chit, before she noticed that I was staring at her.

"18," the chit read.

"How many participants in total?" I asked.

"Eighteen," She replied.

"So, we're last onstage," I said.

"That's self-explanatory," she teased. Her dimple showed again. I blushed.

"What's your name?"

"Shruthi. You are Abhishek. Aren't you?"

"Yeah. How do you know me?" I asked, surprised.

"You were here last year. You won a whole lot of prizes. I was the one who filled up your names in the certificates. You guys are good."

"Thank you."

"You know, you've got some fans too."

"Oh really? Who are they?" I asked, eagerly.

"Well, you're talking to one of them." She smiled. I glanced at her with an evident blush.

"I like that dimple," I said.

"WHAT'S HAPPENING HERE?"

The voice startled both of us. It was Nithin. He stood before us with a serious face, hands folded across his chest.

"Er... ummm. We are last onstage." I faltered, holding the chit up.

"How many participants?" The seriousness was still on his face.

"Eighteen."

"Good. So we have time for a pastry. Come."

"I'll see you around," I told Shruthi, as I was pulled away by Nithin.

Shruthi smiled and waved.

"How cheap!" Nithin said as he walked towards the food counter.

"What's cheap?"

"Flirting with a girl the first time you see her."

"Oh, shut up! I knew what I was doing." I defended myself.

"I don't think so. Don't lose your focus. We have a trophy to win. Excuse me, what's the cost of this?" He asked, pointing at a pastry that was in the display.

"200, per piece sir."

"What? That's expensive." Nithin barked.

"Finally, you manage to stumble on something that is not cheap," I scoffed.

• • •

The light music event began. The first performance was below par. I glanced at my friends.

"We have a chance, guys," I said, giving them a thumbs up.

All the performances that followed were good. Some were mind-blowing. My excitement dropped. So did my friends'.

"Haha! Clean bowled," Nithin mocked.

I glared at Nithin, the convict behind the mess I was in. I glanced back at our team.

"Listen, guys. Let's give it our best shot. It's okay if we don't win."

"Next on stage is Masan Memorial College of Arts and Science."

"Time to rock, mates. Don't forget the strategy we discussed earlier. March ahead. Good luck. Let me go check if I can set some people up to cheer for us. It will add mileage."

I scuttled into the audience as the team stepped on stage.

• • •

The light music event actually turned out to be a stage play competition for the team. They had to act on stage to waste time. Everyone did their job quite well, except Renjith who overdid his role. He walked around the stage scratching his head, thumping his fist and kicking the floor, like a hyperactive cricket bowler whose LBW appeal was just turned down, simply to show that he was unhappy with the keyboard settings.

"Such a pathetic actor," Nithin commented.

"His acting is better than his keyboarding skills though," I joked.

I checked my watch.

"Nice. They've wasted a good four minutes. Two more minutes to go."

Renjith pressed a few keys on the keyboard. The entire crowd, including the judges and the organizers, held their ears against the deafening sound it produced. Renjith gave his team mates thumbs up. I was confused now.

"Now what does that thumbs up mean? Are they going to start? They've got to hold on for a minute at least. And he hasn't even tuned his keyboard properly."

"Wow. The sound is killing. We're so dead," Nithin said.

Renjith had over-tuned the keyboard. Gautham played the guitar for some other song altogether. Vivek suddenly seemed to have forgotten how to sing. The crowd howled. I held my head. All our plans were as off pitch as their singing. The crowd went crazy. They threw paper balls at us. A few people stood on the chairs, tied handkerchiefs around their necks and pretended to be committing suicide. Vivek dropped the mike and ran off stage midway through the song. Sreedev put his flute aside and picked up the mike to continue from where Vivek had stopped. He was welcomed with a few more paper balls. The crowd went crazy. Nithin and I tried to glue ourselves into our seats. It was a bad scene.

We finally managed to croak our way through the entire song. It was time for the instrumental solo now. Ananth started off well. The howling of the crowd slowly came down. He got into a nice flow, and the crowd started grooving to the music. Nithin and I poked our heads out from under the chair. Ananth started enjoying himself. He spun the drumstick around as he played. Suddenly, the snare drum gave way and fell off.

There was a loud "oooooh" from the crowd. Ananth froze. He did not know what to do. We slid our heads back under our chairs. Ananth stopped drumming, bowed in front of the crowd and walked away embarrassed.

I looked at Nithin.

"Out of the auditorium on the count of three," I whispered. "One, two, three."

We lifted our respective chairs and sprinted out of the auditorium with the chairs covering our faces.

• • •

All of us sat under a banyan tree, our heads pointed in different directions, making sure we did not make eye contact with each other. Chalu and Peri walked up towards us after having taken part in cartooning and wall painting respectively.

"What are you guys doing here? They are announcing the results for light music," Peri said.

I glared at Peri with gritted teeth. Peri deciphered the situation.

"How did the off stage events go?" I asked.

"Good. We've done our best," Chalu said.

I noticed Shruthi walking in with a white board that had the points table. She placed the board a few yards away from us and started to write something on it.

"She is cute. I think I should ask her out," I murmured, a little too loudly.

"WHAT???" My friends chorused.

"L-looks like the r-results for light music are out," I said. "Look, she is writing it down."

Shruthi noticed me looking at her. She walked down to me. I took a few steps towards her, away from the guys. I placed my hand on my mouth to ensure I was not drooling.

"Bad start huh?" Shruthi asked.

"Yeah," I said, with a disappointed smile.

"I've got some news that might cheer you up," she said.

I did not answer. I liked listening to her. I had fallen in love with her rich voice and accent. I set my ears up to listen to the good news that was to pass through her bewitching lips.

She came closer to me. Her perfume teased my masculinity. I held my breath and controlled my temptation.

"This is confidential. Okay?"

I nodded.

"I think your college is on the top of the points table at the moment."

My voice box froze. Not only because I was jolted by the good news, but also because I had heard it from an angel who was less than a foot away from me.

"H-How???" That was all my throat could manage.

"You've bagged first places for cartooning and wall painting. They have not announced it yet. So hold your breath until they do."

I did not have any breath to hold. I had lost it the moment she stepped closer to me.

"Okay. I'll catch you later," she said and walked away.

I watched her walk away. Her hair and clothing flying in the breeze. She held her hair and made a neat ponytail with a band she had around her wrist. I was losing focus. The more I watched her, the more I was attracted to her. I could not get rid of the blush on my face. Shruthi disappeared into the auditorium. I turned around to find Peri and Chalu staring at me from either side.

"I am attracted." I shrugged.

Chalu and Peri smiled. I stepped forward and gave them a hug.

"You guys saved us." I shared the private news with all my friends. They were all relieved.

"Let's forget this and concentrate on the other events, guys," I said. "We'll show them what we're capable of."

• • •

Soon the Wizguys were all over the place. We got busy with team registrations, preparations and participation. The competition picked up heat and gradually passed its boiling point. There were a lot of emotions on display—happiness, high-fives, hugs, anger, cheers, disappointment, tears and determination. The crowd was huge. There was a large set of people to cheer for every team. I had a close watch on the points table and also on the lady who updated it. We won prizes for adzap, short film, jam, creative writing, wall painting and cartooning.

The day finally came to its end. The frantic display of talent had to cease. We patiently awaited the results for stick animation, which was the last event of the day. Vivek was not very sure if he had done enough to win. The result came. We didn't make it. There was a loud roar from the supporters of the winning team. We walked out of the auditorium. We had won many prizes, but had we done enough to be on top of the points table?

I glanced at the points table as Shruthi updated it. We were in second place. I shifted my glance towards her. She looked tired. Her *kajal* was smudged around her eyes. Her face appeared dull. She did not seem to bother about her hair anymore. Nevertheless, she still looked stunning. Her bangles clinked merrily against each other as she erased the scores and updated them. I could visualise the marker and the eraser clapping hands and making faces at me. I suddenly began to envy the two lucky non-living creatures. Shruthi turned around after having updated the scores. She noticed me staring at her.

"You're not stalking me are you?" she asked, with a naughty smile.

My soul charged out of me, hugged her tight and kissed her.

"I am," I surrendered.

Shruthi blushed.

"I would like it better if you just came up and spoke to me."

My heart hit me hard as my brain decoded the positivity in the response. I could hear all my organs whispering to me.

"*Come on. Ask her out for dinner. Coffee, atleast. Go right now. Go.*"

I just did not have the courage.

"You look tired," I said.

"You too," Shruthi said.

"I was. But now I am all charged."

Shruthi blushed again. I melted into her dimple. "You're second on the points tally," Shruthi said, trying to change the topic.

"Yup, I am keeping a close watch on the points table," I said. "I really expected to be on top, though."

"Don't worry. You have another day to catch up."

I nodded my head. The disappointment still reflected in my face. Shruthi read my eyes. She took a step closer to me. My lungs stopped working and overworked at the same time.

"Just think logically," she said. "All the big events are happening tomorrow—street play, mime, stage play, western dance, fashion show. You guys are good at all these events. I know because I've watched you closely as a fan."

I just did what I loved doing when she spoke. Sharpen my ears and listen to her. Shruthi took another step closer and held my hand. My heart punched me hard, sending the blood rushing through every vein in my body. Her hand was very soft. She held my hand and took it towards her.

I had a million thoughts racing through my mind. Was she interested in me? Was she going to kiss my hand? Was she going to give me a hug? I closed my eyes and prepared myself to fall prey to the spell of the angel. Shruthi opened her marker and drew a smiley, neatly, on my palm. The wet tip of the marker tickled me.

She let go of my hand. I opened my eyes and looked. I saw the smiley in my hand. My face adapted an expression that conveyed "THAT'S ALL?"

"That's a magic smiley. Don't erase it until you win the trophy tomorrow."

I smiled.

"Good. Keep up that smile. The magic works only if you smile."

I wanted to trust her completely. I had already fallen into her depth. I was drowning in her charm and simply refused to use the life jacket.

"Okay, I've got to go now. Have to make a few arrangements for tomorrow," she said.

"Alright!" I said disappointedly. "See you tomorrow then."

"Sure," she said.

She shook hands with me and walked away. I looked at the smiley in my palm. My smile grew wide.

"Am I in love?" I asked myself. "Or is it just the comprehensible attraction that happens to every normal human?"

I did not care about what it was. I liked the feeling it brought me and decided to live with it that moment.

6
New Year's Eve in the Real World

It took me a while to throw my bad experience with the wrong people in cinema out of my mind. However, I neither failed to look for opportunities nor send endless emails to Shruthi.

It was December 30. While the world made plans for New Year's Eve, I got a call from Chalu. I was surprised to see his call after a long time. He and Peri were working as graphic designers for an MNC in Mumbai.

After a detailed conversation, I learned that they were in Chennai to celebrate the New Year.

"I hope you have not made plans. Let's get together," he said.

I had been battling life all alone for more than a year. The idea of meeting the guys and sharing a few jokes excited me.

"I am in," I said.

"Cool. I'll speak to the other guys too. Will see you tomorrow," he said and hung up.

Just as I made a list of the stuff I wanted to discuss with them the next day, I got a call from director Suresh Lal. This was an unexpected twist, and I answered the call in a hurry, eager to know what he had in store for me.

"Hello, Abhishek. How are you?" he said.

"I am good sir. I hope you are doing fine too." I said. "I am good. I am sorry. I couldn't keep in touch. I was upset that I was associated with the wrong producer. He is a fraud."

"I realised that too, sir," I said.

"Never mind. I am going to work on two projects back to back. A Tamil movie and a Malayalam movie. I have a character for you in both the films."

I waited for him to utter the catch that he had for casting me in his films.

"I might start with the Tamil movie first. Can you come to Gobichettipalayam tomorrow morning? I want to introduce you to the producer."

I was still waiting for the catch. But he appeared to be clean, which meant I had to call Chalu and cancel the New Year's Eve plan and meet him the next day.

"But we are leaving early morning the next day." Chalu said when I talked to him about postponing our meet-up.

I had no choice but to tell him that I would meet him some other day in the future. I couldn't let go of a couple of opportunities that just landed on my lap and Gobichettipalayam it was.

• • •

It was a good ten-hour long journey from Chennai to Gobichettipalayam. I took the night bus and got there by morning. Suresh Lal met me at the bus stand.

"You are bang on time," he said. I did nothing but smile.

"Okay, listen. I am going to meet the producer now. There is a lodge a couple of kilometers from here. Room rates are pretty reasonable there. Get a room and get fresh. The producer and I will meet you in a couple of hours for lunch."

I had no choice but to nod my head. I took an auto rickshaw to the lodge and checked in. As he said, the rate was reasonable, but the room was terrible. It had a single cot that creaked like the doors in horror films. It was probably used as an alarm for those who attempted to have illegal sex on the cot. The fan and the wooden chair screeched in rhythm with the cot, as though they were part of a non-living music band. There was a thin sheet of rusted metal in front of the bathroom, which took part in a fancy dress competition, dressed as a door.

I took a good look around. It wasn't too bad to spend a couple of hours. Just as I settled down, the power went off. When I enquired, I learned that it was a load shedding session and the power would be back on only by evening. I sat on the cot and stared at the wall for more than a couple of hours, waiting to hear from Suresh Lal. Beginning to get impatient, I called him. No answer. Not knowing what to do, I stretched my legs and settled for a nap.

I was woken up by his call a few hours later. I checked the time. It was six in the evening. I couldn't believe I had been asleep for so long.

"I'm sorry, Abhishek. I had a lengthy discussion with the producer. I will be there in twenty minutes."

I freshened up. He came exactly in twenty minutes. "Sorry, buddy. There is a slight change in plan. The producer needs some time to arrange funds. I am thinking of starting with the Malayalam movie."

If the word 'sorry' were some kind of currency, I would have been rich just by the number of apologies he tossed at me.

"What should I do now?" I asked, hiding my frustration.

"You get back to Chennai. I will call you when the Malayalam movie starts."

"Okay, sir," I said, gritting my teeth and thanking him from within for spoiling my chance to meet my buddies after a long time.

• • •

I stared at my mobile phone that still had Shruthi's picture as the wallpaper. It was 11:59 p.m. and I was on the bus on the way back to Chennai. My phone began battling for life. I called home and wished mom, dad and Veena a Happy New Year just as the timer turned to 00:00.

I got a call from Chalu as soon as I hung up. However, my phone switched off the moment I answered the call. I closed my eyes and swallowed my fate, along with the saliva that gathered up in my mouth.

I hoped, like everybody else in the world, for some magic that would make the coming year fruitful for me.

• • •

7

The Magic Smiley

"MAGIC SMILEY?" Chalu and Peri burst into laughter.

Peri, Chalu and I were at Chalu's terrace. The three of us looked worn-out after an exhausting day.

"Shut up! She meant what she said." I turned away from them and sighed. "I haven't been so attracted to any other girl."

"Not even to her?" Peri asked, pointing at Angelynn, who was playing badminton with her friend.

Her terrace was huge with poles erected on the side walls on which strings were attached to hang clothes. Angelynn and her friend used one of those strings as the net for their game. She was wearing a white skin-fit T-shirt with black track pants. She did look hot enough to make anyone's jaw drop. In fact, Peri and Chalu were already speaking to me with dropped jaws. However, I was not interested in looking at her at the moment, which was otherwise one of my favourite pastimes on Chalu's terrace.

"Nope. She does not interest me today."

I glanced at the magic smiley in my hand and smiled as Shruthi instructed me to.

"I guess I have fallen for Shruthi."

"You can't be serious," Chalu said.

"I know. You just saw her today," said Peri.

"Yes, I know. But I really don't know why I am so attracted to her. She is just not leaving my mind. I am in love with this feeling. Let's see how it goes."

Chalu's mom came up to the terrace with three hot cups of tea.

"Why're you guys always on the terrace taking all the mosquito bites? Is this some kind of social service for the mosquitoes?" she asked, as she distributed the cups to the three of us.

"Amma. Abi is in love," Chalu said, causing me to swallow a little too much tea, burning my throat in the process.

"What? No aunty. I-I mean... n-not yet." I stammered.

Chalu's mom was generally friendly with us. She did not mind giving little tips or advice when needed.

"Not yet huh? So there are possibilities that you will fall in love soon? Who is the girl?" she queried.

"He met her at the cultural fest," Peri said.

"Today?" she asked.

I nodded.

"Watch out, Abi. I think it's too fast," she said and started to walk away.

Just then, Angelynn squealed with delight after scoring the winning point. Our heads turned towards her in response to the squeal. Angelynn jumped up and down as though she had just won a gold medal in an Olympic game. Our jaws began to drop again.

"She is HOT!" Peri said, excited.

"WHAT?" Chalu's mom asked as she walked away.

"Ummm... The tea, aunty. It's hot."

Chalu's mom glanced at Angelynn.

"Now I understand why you are feeding the mosquitoes," she teased and walked away.

The three of us laughed. I checked my watch. "Sheesh! It's late. Let me make a move. We've got to get there early tomorrow. The first event is art from waste right?"

"Yes. Who is participating in it? The two of you?" Peri asked.

"Yeah," Chalu replied. "Hey, why don't you guys stay here tonight? We can go together tomorrow."

"I am game." Peri said, immediately.

I took a moment to think. I checked my phone. The battery was almost out. I neither had the charger nor the clothes to wear the next day. Two big reasons to go back home. I looked up at Chalu.

"Okay. I'll stay. But I need answers to three questions," I said.

Chalu and Peri were genuinely confused now.

"What?" Chalu asked.

"Do you have a thin pin Nokia charger?"

"Yes."

"Good. Will you let me wear that black shirt I got you for your birthday?"

"What the hell! Why not?"

"Cool. Will you let me speak about Shruthi for the rest of the night?"

Chalu and Peri exchanged 'red alert' glances.

"No," Peri interrupted. "You can go home."

"You have no choice, brother," I said, gulping down my tea. "Now let's go. I have loads to talk about."

I dragged them from the terrace.

• • •

I sprang from my bed to check the time for what seemed like the hundredth time. I knew the alarm would wake me up, but I did not want to take a chance. I had to get there as early as possible. Not only because I was participating in the first event, but also because I did not want to miss gazing at my newfound sleep-spoiler even with the blink of an eye.

I checked the time with half-open eyes. It was fifteen to six.

"That's it. I am not sleeping anymore." I decided. "Chalu! Wake up. It's time," I said as I towed him out of bed holding his leg.

Chalu peered into his mobile as he was being dragged. "Are you kidding me? It's only five forty five. The night's still young. Shut up and get back to sleep." He whined and crawled back to his cosy patch.

I let out a sigh of hopelessness. I shifted my glance to Peri with a ray of hope.

Peri looked scary while asleep. His eyes were half open with his irises hidden deep under his eye lid. The extent to which his mouth was open was directly proportional to the amount of blockage his nose had.

"Peri," I called.

"Will you fucking let me sleep!" Chalu barked.

I kicked the floor in frustration. I slowly crawled back into bed and lay down in between Chalu and Peri with eyes open as wide as the depleted ozone layer. I glanced at Peri again. He had plugged his ears with cotton as a result of my extensive Shruthi-*jabam* the previous night.

I stared at the ceiling fan as it went round and round and round. I was soon lost in a vortex of thoughts.

"Abbbiiiiii." The voice brought me back to consciousness.

It was Chalu's mom.

"Do you want to have some coffee?"

"Finally someone to talk to," I thought. "I am coming, aunty," I said and glanced at Chalu.

He was missing. I shifted my glance to the other side. Peri still looked scary and was snoring too, to add to the fright. I checked the time. It was seven. My ozone layer depleted wider. I shot out of bed and quickly brushed my teeth.

"Your coffee is on the table, Abi," Chalu's mom shouted from the kitchen.

I picked up the coffee and turned around to find Chalu in his post-honeymoon mode, reading the newspaper with a towel wrapped around his waist.

"Go get ready," Chalu said. "Use the bathroom in my room. I will use the other one. We've got to get there as soon as possible. We can't miss out on any event today."

"Yeah. I'll have to keep a close watch on the points table too," I murmured to myself, as I walked into the bathroom.

I found Chalu's black shirt on the bed beside a frightening Peri. I got dressed and hurried out of the room. To my apprehension, I found Chalu walking to and fro in the living room with his lower half still covered with his long white towel.

"I am going," he said before I could open my mouth to say anything.

• • •

Chalu scurried out of his room dressed in a white shirt and pure white denim jeans as I stuffed the last piece of my third dosa into my mouth.

"You look like a driver," I said with a stuffed mouth. Chalu raised his middle finger. I put my head down and tore a piece off my fourth dosa. Chalu made a swift leap to the dining table, rolled up two dosas and stuffed each of them into his mouth in quick succession.

"Shall we leave?" He asked as he gulped down some water.

"Sure. What about Peri?" I asked, burping.

"He'll find his way. His event is post lunch anyway." Chalu said.

• • •

I kick-started my black Honda Activa and sat on it.

"I'll ride," Chalu said.

"All yours," I said and slid into the backseat. "Now you really are a driver."

"Bad joke," Chalu said, as he raised the accelerator and wheeled the bike out of the parking area.

• • •

It was quarter to nine, and we had covered only half the distance, which meant that we had to cap about eight kilometers in the next fifteen minutes. I was confident that Chalu would make it as he was a fast rider, unlike me.

However, I was on tenterhooks on how the traffic was designed for the day.

"Who has the materials for art from waste?" I asked.

"Nithin will have that covered," Chalu said as he made a sharp bend to avoid a random pit.

Driving in Chennai was like playing a 2D car game. You have to dodge through bizarre obstacles that come your way.

Chalu raced through a good seven kilometers in less than ten minutes. Much to our relief, the traffic was tolerable. We had gotten to the last traffic signal that we had to surpass before we could get to our destination. Chalu honked madly at a few slow starters as soon as the signal turned green.

He took a sudden but swift ninety-degree turn from the traffic signal, setting us up for the final drag towards the finish line. He raised the accelerator. I held the seat tightly. We were almost there.

Chalu cut past a truck and suddenly spotted something that he wished he had noticed at least a second earlier. A drunken man danced in the middle of the street attempting to get to the other side. Chalu pulled the brakes with all the strength his fingers had. The brakes failed to hold the wheel back. Chalu made a frantic turn to avoid a collision with the man. The scooter headed towards the median and BANG.

We found ourselves flying of the vehicle and crash landing on the ground in a matter of seconds.

Chalu held his wrist. I squeezed my knee. We were definitely in severe pain. People crowded around us. A few of them helped us up, while a few others lifted the damaged bike. There was a brief questioning session with common queries like, *"are you hurt?" and "can't you drive safely?"* for which we had to come up with answers.

A large troop of college students stood on the other side of the road. They stood paralysed with their eyes fixed on us as though they had just noticed someone taking a shower right in the middle of the road.

I realised that we were right in front of the Madras Christian College. Nithin, who was one among the spectators of the shower, took his own time to recognise that it was us who were centre stage.

Chalu and I found our way across the street by the time Nithin's feet decoded the message and jostled his way to the front, to come to us.

I looked around, hoping I would spot Shruthi somewhere in the crowd. My eyes kept wandering until I found myself seated in the medical emergency room at the MCC College along with Chalu.

We looked at each other and shared uncomfortable grins.

"Sorry," Chalu said.

"It was not your fault, *machi*," I said.

Meanwhile, the doctor walked in.

"Can't you guys be careful when you are riding?" the doctor asked.

We were hearing this question for the zillionth time. Chalu sighed and cursed the drunken man.

"Let's see what we've got here," the doctor said as he held Chalu's wrist.

Chalu winced in pain.

"Looks like there is a tiny dislocation. We will need an X-ray," he said.

He then walked up to me. I was seated in another chair beside Chalu. He asked me to lie on the cot and examined me. Just then, the door flung open. We turned our heads almost immediately.

My heart sank as I noticed Shruthi standing on the threshold of the medical room, dressed in a deep red pullover and blue jeans, breathing heavily with both panic and pain reflecting in her eyes.

"Yes. How may I help you? Did you meet with an accident too?" the doctor asked.

"Just came to check if everything was okay," Shruthi replied.

"Nothing to fear," the doctor said with an exaggerated smile. "Can you wait outside for some time, dear?"

"Umm... Can she stay, doctor?" I interrupted, just as Shruthi turned around to leave.

"Missing your girlfriend already?" The doctor chuckled. "Come on in."

Shruthi and I blushed at the same time. Shruthi came and sat on a chair beside me. The doctor examined me, as I lay down there with the blush that refused to leave my face.

"Looks like we have a dislocation here as well. Both of you will have to be taken to hospital for an X-ray."

"But we are late for the first event already," I said.

"Abi, I guess you will have to take care of yourself first," Shruthi said.

Chalu glanced at Shruthi. "Excuse me. I met with an accident too," he said.

"W-well both of you," she said.

"Our dislocations can wait till evening," Chalu said and rose from his chair. "Doctor, thank you so much for examining us. We'll take an X-ray and get this treated by the end of the day. Abi, come let's go. We are late for art from waste."

Chalu started to walk away swiftly. I got off the cot and began to walk too.

"Well, I wish you the best of luck then. I will have a couple of bandages sent to you so that you can hold on until evening," the doctor said.

"Thank you, doctor. We would really appreciate that," I said as I limped towards the door.

Shruthi held my hand and placed it around her shoulders. She noticed the magic smiley still intact on my hand.

"Didn't you take a bath today?" she asked.

"Of course, I did." I said, after sniffing my shirt to make sure I smelled alright. "Why do you ask?"

"The magic smiley. It's still there on your hand. As fresh as it was last night."

"How will I let it lose its charm when it has been drawn by an angel?"

"You are a bad flirt," Shruthi said, trying hard not to blush.

We got out of the medical room to find Nithin, Chalu and Renjith standing around us staring at me.

"I-I got to go," Shruthi said. "You take care. Will see you around. All the best."

Shruthi slowly took my hand off her shoulder gently caressing the magic smiley in the process.

"All the best, guys," she wished the three green-eyed boys, who were all ready to pounce on me as soon as she left.

I had to hold off my friends from swarming around me as I watched her walk tenderly into the crowd, her fluffy hair bouncing behind her back with every step she took.

I took my eyes off her as soon as she disappeared into the building opposite to us. I sighed.

"She is adorable. Isn't she?" I said.

"Did you ask her out?" Chalu asked.

"Almost. Wrong time for you guys to have butted in."

"You've got all day, mate. Let's get ourselves registered for the event. We've got to hurry. Nithin, have you brought the materials for art from waste?" Chalu asked, speaking very fast.

"Art from what?" he asked as though he had just landed from Mars and had no clue what language Chalu was speaking.

"Don't tell me you forgot." Chalu said.

"What the hell? You didn't even tell me," Nithin said.

Chalu took his mobile and opened his message inbox. "What the fuck is this then?" he asked holding the mobile right in front of Nithin's face.

Chalu: *Macha don't forget to bring the materials for art from waste.*

Nithin: *Sure. Take care, gorgeous.*

"And why the hell did you call me gorgeous?" Chalu asked, still pissed with him.

Nithin snatched the mobile phone from Chalu and read the message. He then took his mobile phone to recheck. His eyes popped out as he realised the goof-up. He glanced at Chalu and simpered.

"I am sorry. I was messaging someone else. I got confused."

"Perfect!" I said. "Now what are we going to do?"

"You guys appear to be badly hurt. Let me go get the bandages from the doctor," Nithin said and disappeared from the vicinity.

Chalu and I glanced at each other, our eyes explaining how clueless we were.

"Guys, if you don't mind, can I register for this event?" Renjith asked.

"We don't even have materials. What are you going to do there?" I asked.

"Don't bother too much about that. I will just need some newspapers, water, glue and paint. Besides, I think the both of you should take a breather. We've got bigger events lined up for the day."

I envisioned the idea of getting some rest beside the scoreboard. The thought kindled me, but I was not sure if I should put the trophy at risk.

"Are you sure you can take care of this?" I double-checked.

"You can definitely bet your money on me," Renjith reassured me. "I'll take Nithin with me. You guys chill."

"NITHIN!" Renjith shouted at the top of his voice, as he walked towards him, trying to grab his attention from the food counter, the area to which he had absconded.

"I hope he wins," I said.

"I am apprehensive after witnessing all the drama he created at the light music event yesterday," Chalu said.

I glanced at my watch.

"Okay, we've got a good one hour to spare. Let me go practise my proposal scene," I said and marched ahead without even waiting for Chalu's response.

"Good luck, traitor!" Chalu screamed.

I raised my hand in acknowledgement as I limped towards the scoreboard area.

• • •

We had a very productive day. Renjith had surprised us with a gold medal, in the art from waste event.

"My sweet lord of surprises, what did you do with those newspapers?" I asked, unable to pull back my eyeballs that were hanging out now.

"I mashed the paper with water, added glue and did some paper modelling."

We stared at him, all sharing the incomprehension equally among us.

"You know, when you mash paper with water and add glue, you can kind of use it for modelling, just like clay modelling."

I was still surprised.

"From where did you pick that idea up?"

"Perks of watching Pogo with my little niece," Renjith said, beaming with pride.

Our team had also secured places in numerous other events such as street play, mime, western dance and adaptune. However, the points that we had scored still did not take us to the top of the board. We were still ten points behind the competitive SRM University, which meant we had to win first place in the fashion show, whatsoever to clinch the overall title.

• • •

We were in the classroom allotted to us for dressing up for the fashion show event. The entire team, including the girl participants Sharon, Monica, Aarthi and Parvathi, were present. The girls were already dressed in their heavy conceptual costumes.

Sharon was dressed in a cream-coloured skin-fit gown, which had a thick bushy floral bottom that looked like the wooden leftovers of a sharpened pencil.

Monica looked adorable in a blue mermaid costume that perfectly matched her hourglass shape.

Aarthi's costume was a little too experimental. She fixed herself inside a large inverted paper cup that was brownish. The attire looked like a stiff long frock, which covered her completely from shoulder to feet, except for her sleeveless arms that jutted out of the sides of the cup. The cup had the word 'COFFEE?' written on it.

Parvathi was wrapped in a confusing one-piece, which had film strips hanging down from around her knees.

"Nithin, how are the points for fashion show going to be?" I asked as I removed my shirt revealing my shaved bare body.

Nithin coughed as he poured excess water into his throat from the bottle of water he was drinking, as soon as the question was shot at him.

"Similar to the other events. 100 for first place, 60 for second place and 30 for third," Peri replied before Nithin could take out the rules brochure again and read out the rules for face painting or any other event but the fashion show.

"So that means we have to make sure we win the first place to get to the cup. It doesn't matter if SRM wins second because we would still be 30 points ahead of them," I said as I made a rough calculation in my head.

"Ummm... there is also a Prince and Princess title, which will carry 50 points each," Nithin said, with a sarcastic grin, after making sure he was reading out the content from the fashion show section of the rules brochure.

I snatched the brochure from Nithin and re-confirmed, not wanting to trust him completely.

"Oh fuck!!! This can be tricky." I took out my imaginary book and pen again.

"Okay. So now if SRM wins the second place and both the Prince and Princess titles." I took a moment to calculate. "We will be screwed. We've got to win the first place and also win at least one title to get the cup."

"Now will you please stop your probability calculations and remove your pants so that we can start working on you," Sharon said.

"Oh yeah, we've got to buck up," I said and hesitantly removed my pants, exposing my entire body except for the boxers that covered my centre and the bandage that covered my knees.

I was to decorate my bottom half with a saree that had complicated frill work. The upper porion of my body was to be left bare, only with tattoos across my chest and arms.

Sharon wrapped the saree around my waist and skillfully worked her fingers through the saree, creating seamless frills, while Monica and Aarthi started drawing tattoos on my chest and arms with markers.

"Lucky bastard," Nithin shouted. "Do you want me to take your place, Abi? I am not sure if you will be able to walk the ramp with an injured knee. Aarthi, I want a tattoo on my biceps too." He yapped aimlessly, holding up his three-day gym lump.

"Shut the fuck up, Nithin. I am losing concentration here," she yelled.

"You know what Aarthi, I pity the fact that you will not be able to sit down with that costume on," Nithin said, indicating her stiff paper cup dress and of course not giving a damn about shutting up.

Aarthi flung the marker at him. Nithin ducked reflexively, causing the marker to go further and land on Shruthi, who had just walked into the room.

Aarthi gasped. Nithin turned around to check what made her gasp.

"I am sorry," Aarthi said.

"No problem. Pretty dress," Shruthi replied.

"You call that a dress? She looks like a 3D Coffee Day logo," Nithin attempted to joke.

"Don't mind him, Shruthi. What's up?" I asked, still stuck in between the two ladies who were drawing designs on me.

"Nothing. I just came to check if this is the final list of names for the fashion show," she said, unable to take her eyes off me.

"Nithin... no not you... Peri, can you please check," I asked.

Peri glanced at the paper, while Shruthi kept her eyes on my costume and the ladies around me.

"Abi, what is this?" Monica asked, noticing Shruthi's magic smiley on my hand.

"Oh. That's ummm..." I looked at Shruthi, who glanced back at me with naughty eyes. "That's another tattoo," I said.

"We've got to remove it Abi. It does not look good."

Shruthi frowned the moment she said that. She snatched the paper from Peri and walked away in a huff.

"Sh-shruthi!" I called as she made a dramatic exit. My face turned pale. I took a gander at the magic smiley and then glanced at Monica. There was a moment of silence in the room. Everybody had their eyeballs set on me as though I was accused of murder and was waiting for my head to be chopped off.

"Is there a problem, Abi?" Monica queried.

"Well, I don't know yet," I sighed. "But that can wait. Let's concentrate on our only hope of clinching the trophy."

• • •

The last and the most anticipated event of the evening started off in grand style much to the excitement of the people in the auditorium. Students gathered around the ramp, pushing each other out of the way to get the closest seats possible so that they would not miss the tiniest moment of the most glamorous event.

The stage was decorated with a contemporary fashion theme that looked like a discotheque.

I looked at the long ramp on which I had to walk without showing the slightest sign of a possible knee dislocation. There were three judges—two ladies and a gentleman, who were into fashion and who definitely looked like they knew a lot about the fashion industry.

"Are we ready to rock and roll?" An unidentified voice called through the loud speakers.

"Yeeaaaaaaaaaahhhh!" The auditorium quaked.

My heart started pumping rapidly the moment the announcement was made. We were backstage taking a look at the stage and the ramp and memorising our positions.

"We're going to rock, guys," I said, giving each team member a fist bump.

The show began. Every participant looked attractive and appeared as though they would run away with all the accolades.

The entire arena shuddered with the deafening roars of the students for the next couple of hours. It was as though someone had accidentally set their television at maximum volume and lost the remote control.

The sizzling ladies, who walked the ramp, gathered more noise than the men, who had to struggle to increase the decibel level.

"Next on stage, team Masan Memorial."

The announcement was made. The supporters cheered. Shruthi quickly moved from the front row to a chair beside the judges to get a clear view of me, her newfound infatuation.

Masan Memorial started off with Monica and I walking down the ramp. We posed, turned around, took a few steps and turned around again to strike a reverse pose. The crowd went crazy. Monica retained her position while I walked back and hit the ramp again with Aarthi. We reached the edge of the ramp and blew flying kisses to the students.

Shruthi ducked to let Aarthi's flying kiss pass above her for the others to gobble up and quickly caught hold of my kisses, making sure she did not let any of them go past her. She placed it safely on her cheek and blew a flying kiss back at me.

Aarthi stepped to another position, while I came back with Sharon. The crowd went berserk, and so did Shruthi.

The atmosphere remained electrifying until the last participant walked down the ramp of glamour. The team round was over, and it was now time for the Prince and Princess rounds.

The Wizguys in the crowd screamed with delight when they heard that Sharon and I were selected for the next round. However, our excitement dropped as soon as they announced the names Varun and Devika, the contestants from SRM College, who were also selected.

"This is going to be crazy," Sharon said, biting her nails.

"Just chill and do your best. We are going to win," I said, giving Sharon a thumbs up.

Sharon, Devika, Varun, me and a couple of other contestants waded through the next few rounds to reach the final round.

Devika looked tantalising in her long white Egyptian robe that could steal the gazes of many. Her blue eyes were her USP, which she knew very well and made the best use of.

"I must admit, she looks hot," I whispered to Sharon as we stood backstage waiting to be called on stage.

"I hate you," Sharon said, elbowing my stomach playfully.

"I request the participants to come onstage," one of the female judges announced.

She had long straightened hair that was left loose. She wore dark pink lipstick that complemented her fair complexion. She was dressed in a blue sleeveless top and a long white slit skirt that exposed her beautiful and shining legs. The massive heels that she wore added to the enticement of her legs.

We took deep breaths and stepped onstage along with the others, who also made nervous entries.

The auditorium erupted as soon as we appeared in front of them. The judges glanced at us with broad smiles, holding the results of the winners on their scoring pads.

"Great show all of you. And we've got the results right here," the female judge said.

We glanced at each other.

"Nervous?" she asked.

A few of the others just smiled anxiously while I nodded my head indicating I was nervous.

"Alright, here we go. In the team round. Third place goes to Women's Christian College."

The beautiful ladies of Women's Christian College screamed in delight.

"Second place – SRM College of Arts and Science."

Some supporters of SRM cheered, while some held back their enthusiasm as they knew that they would be in trouble if we won first place.

I made a rough calculation in my mind.

SRM – 510 + 60 = 570

MASAN – 500

"Any guesses for the first place?" The judge shouted through the mike.

I glanced at Sharon, who was with me onstage. Sharon closed her eyes. Shruthi crossed her fingers and tried to peek into the scorecard that the judge was holding. There was a moment of silence.

"First place goes to Masan Memorial College of Arts and Science," the judge screamed through the mike.

I jumped with delight. Sharon hugged me. There were loud cheers and audible high-fives doing the rounds. I brought out my imaginary score card again.

SRM – 570

MASAN – 500 + 100 = 600

The female judge placed her mike on the table. The male judge picked his mike up now.

He was dressed in a white skin-fit T-shirt and brown corduroy pants along with a maroon scarf wrapped around his neck. He had spiked hair and wore more accessories than men generally would.

"Alright. Now it's time for the individual rounds. I've got the name of a Princess and a Prince right here before me. I will read out the name of the Princess, while this beautiful lady beside me will announce the Prince." He said pointing at the second lady judge who looked pretty in her backless pink dress.

"The Princess tonight is... Devika from SRM College."

Devika squealed as though she was crowned Miss Universe. Sharon heaved a sigh of worry. I held Sharon's arm in an attempt to console her and simultaneously reopened my scorecard.

SRM – 570 + 50 = 620

MASAN – 600

The judge walked up on stage with a crown and placed in on Devika's head. The SRM supporters celebrated.

"Ladies and gentlemen, can we hold back our excitement for just a bit? We also have a Prince here tonight." The other female judge said, amid the pandemonium in the auditorium.

The uproar came down gradually. Every person in the auditorium already had an answer in their mind.

"Is it going to be Varun Shankar of SRM, Nivaz Ahmed of New College or Abhishek Krishnan of Masan Memorial?" the judge said as she glanced at her scorecard with a smile, obviously knowing who the winner was.

I clenched Sharon's hand tightly. The supporters of Masan and SRM filed applications to their respective gods. The collective sounds of each one's heartbeat turned out to be the perfect background music for the situation.

"And the winner is Abhishek Krishnan from Masan Memorial College of Arts and Science."

I raised my hands in triumph and struck a victory pose. Sharon hugged me and lifted me to the extent she could.

SRM – 620

MASAN – 650

"We have made it, Abi!" Sharon shrieked in glee. Meanwhile, the judge came up on stage to crown me.

The entire Masan Memorial team came up onstage and smothered me. It was indeed time to rejoice after all the hard work, screw ups and the pain we went through.

I squeezed my way out of the crowd with my costume half damaged. I waded through the mess in the auditorium, holding on to my costume and headed towards the changing room.

The corridor ahead of me was long, empty and dark. My friends seemed to have thrown off their weighty attires the moment the team round was over. I held my costume and slowly walked down the narrow pathway, happy not only about the fact that we won the overall trophy, but also because I could now limp according to my free will after all that painful pretentiousness on the ramp.

As I tottered weakly down the corridor, I heard the faint sound of anklets that echoed down the length of it. I stopped to realise that the sound grew louder as though someone was nearing me. I turned around and found Shruthi running towards me, her cheeks redder than her red pullover.

I waited for her to catch up.

"Great show, Prince," Shruthi said as she gasped for breath.

"Thank you, Princess," I replied.

Shruthi blushed. I stared at Shruthi as though I had all the permission to.

"Do you own the patent rights for the colour red by any chance?" I asked as we started walking down the corridor.

Shruthi looked at me, her eyes explaining her incomprehension.

"Red T-shirt, red sandals, red nail polish... oh, you've also got some nice red lipstick," I said after taking a close look at her lips.

Shruthi's cheeks reddened. "There you go. Red cheeks too," I teased. "You were in red yesterday as well."

"That was cherry red. This is chestnut red. They are two different colours," Shruthi said.

I laughed.

"I am amazed by the way you girls identify different shades of colours," I said.

"And I am amazed by the way you managed to pull up so much support at the fashion show," she said.

"It's a trick," I whispered. "It's quite obvious that the girls gather maximum sound when they hit the ramp. So we choreographed the walk in such a way that one of the boys in our team strides down with all four girls at a stretch."

"... and that boy was you." Shruthi said, as though she was solving a jigsaw puzzle.

"Yes! We took a gamble this time," I replied. "So when the crowd cheers for the pretty girls who walk with me, a portion of the crowd is deceived. And the next time they see me on the ramp, they automatically cheer for me, and it gets contagious."

"Impressive," Shruthi said, clapping her soft hands. "And your trick has won you the overall trophy."

I stopped walking as I reached the threshold of the dressing room. I turned towards Shruthi and looked into her angelic eyes.

"It's not the trick," I said in a deep voice. "It's this."

I stretched my hand before Shruthi to reveal the magic smiley still intact. Shruthi's eyes sparkled as she saw it.

"Awwwww. You still have it. That's so cute. I thought you would have removed it when your partner asked you to."

"How could I remove the lucky charm of a fairy!" I said with a lot of passion.

Shruthi's brown eyes swooped into mine. She took a few steps closer to me, her warm breath hit my bare chest. She held my hand and kissed the magic smiley. The warmth of her lips tingled through my body.

"I-I got to go change. C-catch you later," I stuttered nervously and escaped into the room.

I locked myself inside and held my head, breathing heavily.

"Why are you so nervous, Abi?" I asked myself. "She is a girl and she has the guts to take the first step. You have definitely made her feel bad. Get dressed, go find her and apologise to her."

I calmed myself, got dressed quickly and opened the door to leave. As I opened the door, I noticed Sharon standing right outside, still dressed in her fashion show outfit, and with her was Shruthi, who was in the midst of a random conversation with Sharon.

"Sh-sharon, what are you doing here?" I stammered, not knowing what to say.

"Duh! We share the same dressing room. I can't be going back home dressed like this," Sharon sneered.

"Oh yeah, of course. Go ahead." I said. As soon as Sharon went inside and shut the door, I glanced at Shruthi nervously. She glanced back at me with a nervous smile.

"Abi, I want to show you something," she said, saving me from the awkwardness.

She put her hand inside a little bag that she carried and took out a small diary that looked more like a scrapbook. She handed the book over to me, her face revealing her fear.

My brain quickly prepared a question paper for which I knew no answers. I opened the book anxiously and found many collages of my pictures that were taken during the same cultural program the previous year. I flipped through the pages and found pictures of myself in different emotional states—happy, sad, excited, nervous and triumphant. On the last page of the book were written the words.

In your laughter, I smile.
In your grief, I cry.
In your nervousness, I chew my nails.
In your triumph, I celebrate.

My eyes slipped through the words. I glanced at Shruthi, dumbstruck by what I saw.

"I just could not take my eyes off you last year. I first thought it was just some kind of an infatuation," Shruthi said, after clearing her throat multiple times, as the words did not come out. "So I held back my emotions and waited one full year to see if my feelings were genuine."

She took a moment to calm her heartbeat, which had started to kick her rib cage.

"Well... here I am... standing before you... still carrying all the feelings I had for you a year ago."

"I love you, Abi," she said, getting on her knees.

I was completely dumbfounded. I was floored. I stood there standing before the girl I met just a day ago, witnessing one of the best and boldest proposals by any girl in the history of love proposals. I went down on my knees too, quickly reacting to her action, my eyes welling up uncontrollably. I held her by her arm and lifted her to her feet.

"Shruthi... I... I... you know... I don't know..." I just did not know what to say.

Shruthi placed her fingers to my lips.

"Ssshhhhh..." She whispered. "I did not ask you for an answer. It took me one full year to decide whether I was really in love with you. I know you aren't sure yet. I just wanted to express my feelings for you. I will completely understand if you do not have the same feelings for me. We'll be in touch, and if you ever fall in love with me, I will be the happiest girl on earth."

"Shruthi. You look stunning. I-I fell for you the moment I saw you," I said. "I like you, but I am not sure if I am really in love with you. I am glad you understand my situation."

Shruthi smiled as she examined my face, running her eyes over my eyes, cheeks and lips.

"Abi...," she said.

"Yes..."

There was a moment of silence.

"Ummm ... C-can I k-kiss you?" she asked reluctantly. "What if you never fall in love with me? This might be our first and last kiss."

I blushed. I was cornered by the boldness and ingenuity of the pretty lady in front of me. I angled my cheek towards her almost immediately and anticipated the touch of her lovely red lips on my cheek.

Shruthi held my chin. I could feel the tender touch of her fingers, as her beautiful long nails caressed my skin. She turned my face towards hers and planted her lips on mine before I could realise what happened.

I held her tightly, as I fell victim to the intensity of her tender lips, after assuming in the back of my mind that

Sharon was still changing and was not going to open the door to ruin my first ever kiss.

I looked into her eyes as soon as our lips parted. There was a mixed sense of contentment and hopefulness in them. Content that she finally expressed herself. Hopeful about a positive response. I was blown away by the fact that she had waited a full year just to make sure that her feelings for me were genuine. I was pretty sure she would never ever leave me. But how much longer was I going to make her wait?

• • •

8

The Bag of Hopes and Dreams

I waited. I waited for Shruthi's reply. I waited for a call from Suresh Lal. I waited for an opportunity. I pushed away job vacancies that came my way, as I thought I wouldn't be able to step away from work in case Suresh called me all of a sudden like he usually did. My frustration grew along with the mounting responsibilities at home. I did small designing and writing jobs to make ends meet. My parents began to get impatient. They started to pressurise me to quit cinema and look for a job. I kept consoling them saying success wasn't too far away.

Suresh Lal finally called me. I was glad that he did not forget the promise he made.

"Abhishek, the Malayalam project has finally started," he said.

"Oh, that's great news, sir," I said.

"Yes. I am working on the script. I need help with it. It is in Tamil. I want someone to translate the entire thing into Malayalam. Do you know anyone who can do this for me? The pay will be good," he said.

Now, this looked like an opportunity for me as I could read and write both languages. Moreover, I could make some money doing something I liked.

"Sir, can I take it up?" I asked.

"Well of course." He sounded delighted. "It is always good to work with someone you are comfortable with. You also have a character in the film. You can work with us and leave after the shoot."

It sounded like a good deal to me.

"When and where do I have to come?" I asked, excitedly.

"Kozhikode. You'll have to start tomorrow night. The producer is in a hurry to launch the movie as soon as possible."

"So am I," I told myself.

• • •

"See, I told you I would have to leave any moment. That is why I rejected that job offer," I told *amma*, as I put on my socks.

I was in a hurry to leave. As it was too short a notice, I did not get a reservation on a train. I had to travel in the general compartment, which meant I had to get there as early as possible to get a seat. I packed a couple of chapatti rolls that *amma* made, along with clothes for at least a month's stay. I somehow felt this would be a turning point in my career. Along with the bag of food and clothes, I carried with me a few pinches of hope that I carefully placed in the side pouch of my travel bag.

"Bye, *amma* See you in around a month." I said.

"Take care. Call me once you get there," she said.

"Sure ma. Tata."

I could feel *amma* praying hard for me as I walked out of the house. The positive vibes of her prayer touched and blessed me. I could feel her looking at me as I walked away. But I did not want to turn and glance back at her as I felt I would get emotional. Although she kept asking me to get a job and start earning some regular income, I knew very well that she silently wished from her heart that I conquer my dream someday.

I could understand her frustration and worry. She obviously wanted her son to fare well and have a good reputation in society. I could understand she hated the sympathetic comments and advice I got from our relatives. I was glad she held her nerve for me all these days. I was pacified that the long wait had been worthwhile and I was sure *amma* felt the same too.

• • •

I poked through the crowd as the train arrived. It was an overnight journey to Kozhikode, and I had to find a seat. I laughed in triumph from within when I managed to jump into the train before anyone else could, as it arrived.

I stepped into the train with a determined mindset to grab the best seat in the compartment. But to my astonishment, I found all the seats occupied already. My eyes popped out.

How did these people manage to enter the compartment before the train even arrived?

By the time I walked the length of the compartment hoping to find an empty seat, the crowd behind me had swarmed in, and in no time we were all breathing carbon dioxide mixed with sweat.

I placed my bag by the door and stood by it. All I could do was shift my standing position when my legs hurt. Just as the train began to leave, another huge pack of people pounced in through the door like wolves, snatching away my freedom to move, breathe or hold onto something.

The smell of sweat and the odour from the toilets enhanced my breathing. People were screaming, hooting and chatting away liberally, their vocal chords tormenting my ear drums.

People with high sugar and cholesterol took evening walks within the compartment every now and then, piercing themselves through us on their way, not letting us settle into a comfortable posture.

On one such instance, I lifted my foot to assist someone walk past me to answer nature's call. But when I placed it back, I realised that the little space that my foot occupied had been taken away. I attempted to place my foot on someone else's, but their cold stare made me think otherwise, forcing myself to stand on one leg for a good half an hour until I struck a deal with a boy from Delhi who was standing on one leg too.

"You rest your foot on mine for fifteen minutes, and I'll place mine on yours for the next fifteen minutes," he said.

Although it was the most disastrous deal I had ever made in my life, my aching leg begged me to accept it. Our deal went strongly for a good couple of hours. We used stop watches to make sure we exchanged foot placements every fifteen minutes. I was glad I wore shoes, as the weight of his leg was as unbearable as his boring stories of his encounters with winter in Delhi.

After a couple of stations, a few people got off the train. I found a little breathing space around me, while the Delhi winter survivor managed to strike a deal with someone else and got hold of a seat.

I gobbled up the chapatti rolls *Amma* had packed and stood leaning against the wash basin, my eyes forcing shut every now and then.

By the time I reached Kozhikode the next morning, I was craving some sleep. My legs went on strike, going numb, refusing to walk or stand anymore.

I waddled towards a chair at the railway station and collapsed in it. I wanted to find a bed and crash as soon as possible. I pulled my phone out and called Suresh Lal. My eyes sleepily travelled across the railway station as I anticipated the sound of the ring.

"Beep. Beep. Beep. Thaangal vilikkunna number switch off cheythirikukayanu. The number you have called is currently switched off."

My brain almost jumped out of my skull as soon as my ear transferred the recorded message to it. It pleaded with my ears to send it a positive sound wave.

Fuck!!!!!! I yelled in my head.

I tried a couple more times. Switched off. I almost threw my phone away in frustration. I was furious and messed up by the situation I had been in since the previous night. I did not even have the energy to curse him. I took a deep breath and consoled myself.

"Okay, Abi. He must be held up somewhere without battery charge. Just relax. He'll call you in a while." I told myself.

I decided to wait and in the process I dozed off leaning on the chair, clinging tightly to my luggage. I forced open my eyes every four minutes hoping to get him on the line. After about four hours, I got a call from a local Kozhikode number. It was him.

"I'm sorry, Abhishek. I was drunk last night. I left my mobile phone at the bar."

There you go. Another expensive sorry spent. I just needed a few more of them to build a house. He always had a fresh excuse attached to his apology. He must have had been purchasing them in pairs.

"It's okay, sir," I said.

Well, it definitely was not okay."Where are you?" He asked.

"At the railway station, sir. Waiting for your call."

"Oops. Okay. I'll send you a pick-up car."

"Okay sir. I'll wait," I said, hoping that he wouldn't call back and toss another sorry-excuse pair at me.

The pick-up arrived in ten minutes much to my relief. My body screamed in happiness as I lifted my luggage and put it in the boot. The pinches of hope that I carried in the side pouch decided to stay.

• • •

We stayed at a guest house on the outskirts of Kozhikode, far away from the crowd and noise. During my stay, a lot of industry friends – from make-up men and assistant directors to cinematographers and script writers met Suresh Lal at the guest house to enjoy a little down time. While I worked on the script, they discussed their experience working on various movies—the ego clashes they had, the locations they went to and the different perverted ideas they used to lure women and have sex with them.

An elderly make-up man, who was around sixty years of age, narrated the story of how he managed to convince an innocent junior artist into sex. He made her believe that her bust was too small and that women needed bigger breasts to get better roles in cinema. He apparently gave her a bottle of oil claiming that it was some kind of a size enhancer. He offered to massage it onto her bust himself, and ultimately seduced her into sex.

The worst thing about the story was that he narrated it with a lot of pride, as though he had saved the Prime Minister of the country from terrorists.

The film industry definitely isn't a hundred percent clean. Like any industry, it has its share of bad and good people. I wanted to be one among the best set of people. But I had to get into films in the first place. I wanted to concentrate on that instead of letting my mind drift away by stories such as these.

Suresh sir had explained to me the character I was to be playing. I checked the depth of the role in the script. It was a good one. I was delighted.

• • •

It took me a month to translate the entire script to Malayalam. They were going to change the sequences and dialogues according to the taste of the audience in Kerala. I had to translate the Tamil words and dialogues in the script into Malayalam so that they could read and work on it.

"Okay, Abhishek. I guess you can head back to Chennai and take some rest. I'll let you know our shooting dates," Suresh sir said.

I really needed that break to go back home and prepare. "Sure, sir. Where are we going to shoot?"

"Ooty, Delhi and Goa."

"Sounds good, sir. I'll book my train tickets to Chennai for the earliest date available," I said.

"You can book one for today evening. The producer will help you get a reservation," he said.

I nodded my head.

"*That sounds better*," I thought.

"And make sure you get your payment from him." That sounded even better. I nodded and smiled.

By evening the producer handed me a train ticket with a confirmed berth and one thousand five hundred rupees, which was supposed to be my payment for playing the role of an over-exploited Tamil to Malayalam dictionary for a month.

I did not understand in which note, among the fifteen hundred rupee notes, Suresh Lal's 'the pay will be good' statement existed.

I was disappointed but did not want to express it as I knew that the movie would be a turning point for me considering the depth of the character I was going to play.

The signal on the railway track turned green. The train began to move. It was a definite green signal for my career. The pinches of hope I carried began to grow.

• • •

It took four months for Suresh Lal to call me. Every time I called him, he would say that the project would commence in a week's time, thus extending the validity of my hope by seven days.

I ignored the stares of hopelessness from my parents and relatives. I tried to avoid family get-togethers. I was fed up with the Kathakali expressions my face made when someone asked me what I was doing.

The old people in the family advised me to look for a government job while the younger ones irked me by displaying their credit cards and the gadgets they got with their own thick salaries.

I never missed an opportunity to stare at my mobile phone waiting for Suresh Lal to call. All I received was a smile from Shruthi who still taunted me as my wallpaper and of course the constant service and sales calls.

Finally, after showing my mobile phone my desperate face for four months, he called. My soul ran to my laptop and prepared itself to book tickets to the destination he would utter in a few minutes. Suresh Lal started with what he was an expert at – an excuse and a sorry.

A sorry for not calling.

An excuse that they were waiting for the dates of a big hero.

However, the sorry did not stop with just one this time round.

“I am sorry, Abhishek. I have planned to drop this project. I’ve suddenly lost interest in the movie. But I will be starting the Tamil project in a couple of months for sure,” he said.

I was mind-fucked. He had been playing ping-pong with my hopes for quite a while now. My mind had two choices of answers for him.

I had two options: either ask him to fuck off or simply swallow my anger and tell him I would wait for the Tamil movie project to commence. I chose the latter.

What was I doing wrong? Why was I being pulled off the ladder to success every time I neared the top? Why did success seem so near yet so far? How would I console my parents? What dance form should I practice to give my relatives an answer? Why me? Why me all the time?

• • •

I did not have high hopes for Suresh Lal's Tamil movie. The pressure at home began to steam through my ears. I searched for jobs crazily on the internet. There were many. But all of them demanded a registration charge. I didn't mind paying. However, some of the reviews suggested that they were all frauds and I was tired of dealing with a sufficient number of frauds.

Fortunately, I managed to find an animation company that was planning to do a cartoon series. I did screenplays for them. The pay was decent, and I could concentrate on hunting for film opportunities too, as this was part-time.

• • •

My wild hunt in a forest full of traps continued for about five months, and suddenly one fine day Suresh Lal called.

"Abhishek, how are you?" he asked.

"I am good, sir." I did not bother to ask if he was fine.

"I am in Chennai at the moment. Can we meet?"

I remained silent for a while.

Was this going to be another silly story? I thought. *But what if he had a project in hand and wanted to give me a role?*

As a desperate aspirant, I always tended to push my hope into any minuscule crack available. I decided to stay positive.

"Sure sir. When?" I asked.

"Like now? I am at the Koyambedu bus stand."

• • •

I reached the bus stand in ten minutes. I met him at the entrance. He appeared to be tired and worn out as though he had pushed the bus all the way to Chennai. He was in a black shirt and jeans. He had grown a beard along with some extra flab around his waist and was barefoot. By his appearance, I guessed he was fasting for Sabarimala.

People are earnest about their fasting for Sabarimala in India. It is believed that Lord Ayyappa lived in Sabarimala, where his temple exists now. Devotees fast for forty-one days before going to the temple. During the fasting period, they wear black clothes, refrain from eating non-vegetarian food, leave their beards and hair unshaved or untrimmed, walk around barefoot, stay away from alcohol, do not have sex, speak the truth and don't participate in fraudulent acts.

If he was actually fasting, I could take my chances with trusting him as the probability of him telling a lie was at the bare minimum.

"Abhishek, I was drunk in the bus last night. Someone stole my wallet," he said.

The Sabarimala Swami in my mind jumped out and dove into a pool of hopelessness, providing me with near accurate answers to his current state.

Beard - Laziness

Extra flab - Drinking too much

Bare feet - Must have lost his footwear along with his wallet.

Black attire - Just a stupid coincidence

"I am supposed to meet a producer today. Can you lend me two thousand rupees? I'll return it to you by tomorrow," he said.

I had the money he asked for, but I did not want to lend it to him. I knew I would neither get it back nor was it going to be used for anything constructive.

"I'm sorry sir. I am totally broke," I said.

"Can you ask your friends?" he said.

"I already owe them a lot of money."

"Can I pledge your watch for money?" he asked, noticing the Rolex I wore, which Shruthi had gifted me during our green days.

I began to get irritated.

"Not possible. This is not mine. The most I can do is drop you at the place you intend to go," I said, sounding slightly irked.

I wasn't bothered anymore about the movie prospects he might have had for me. I wanted to get rid of him, the earlier, the better.

"Can you drop me at Kodambakkam?" he asked, overlooking my irritation.

Kodambakkam is probably the home of Tamil cinema. Many production houses, dubbing studios, movie equipment units, costumes and all other movie-related stuff exists in that long stretch between Kodambakkam and Vadapalani. Aspiring actors, directors and other technicians spend hours in the tea shops in Kodambakkam, sipping away gallons of tea and discussing scripts, hoping to climb the wall of fame someday.

I dropped Suresh Lal at his friend's house in Kodambakkam and sped away, without bothering to say bye. I had just thrown away a contact that I so foolishly believed was a prospect. When I looked back at those frustrating months of waiting, I could see Suresh Lal waving at me with a grin on his face. The kind of grin one would wear when they outsmart you, exploiting your money, energy and time.

I had to build a new contact and an opportunity. But the question was – where do I start?

• • •

9

Shruthi

"What?"

"You serious?"

"How?"

"When?"

"Where?"

Peri and Chalu were shooting rapid-fire questions at me, one after the other, not giving me time to let air pass through my nostrils.

The three of us were at our headquarters, facing each other, forming an obtuse triangle under the moonlight, after banging our heads through the after-party of a victorious day. Chalu and I had also examined our possible elbow and knee dislocations and were relieved to find that there was nothing serious.

During my one-hour-long narration of the gamut of events that took place post the fashion show, a few lights in the neighbourhood were turned off, the moon finally found freedom from a dark patch of clouds, the mosquitoes were halfway through their list of casualties for the night, and Angelynn had won four straight sets against her little brother.

However, neither her brand new track suit nor her squeals of victory at the stroke of midnight attracted the attention of the guys as my story had more content in it.

"Dude, are you crazy?" Peri said, trying to hold back his long hair from falling into his eyes. "You've been chanting her name since yesterday. Why didn't you accept her proposal?"

"Why are you overreacting now?" Chalu asked Peri, in an attempt to defend me. "*Macha*, it's good that you have taken time to think about it. The night is still young. Think about it while we watch this last set of night badminton."

"And if you think you need more time, you can take as much as you want when we are asleep," Peri added, with a grin.

"There is no way I am spending the night here. I need to be clean-shaven and well-dressed when I meet Shruthi tomorrow."

"Well, looks like someone's made a decision," Chalu said.

"Oh yes, I have," I said, winking.

• • •

I ran into a tall hotel building, holding Shruthi's hand tightly.

"Abbi, where are you taking me?" Shruthi screeched with curiosity as she was pulled into the empty elevator.

I loosened my grip on her hand as soon as the door closed. Shruthi's eyes shouted a thousand questions. As she opened her mouth to speak, I grabbed her and locked my lips with hers. She placed her hands on my chest in a half-hearted attempt to push me away, but instead gradually clenched my shirt with the intensity of the kiss as I pulled her closer to me.

The elevator reached the twelfth floor, the topmost in the building. I took my lips off Shruthi's like the doors un-kissed each other. I carefully lifted her light body in my arms and walked up the flight of stairs that led to the terrace. Her footwear tapped her heels with every step I took causing her thin anklets to ring a sweet melody.

The terrace was empty and large. There was a huge water tank on the terrace that had an iron ladder beside it to get on top of it. I carefully placed Shruthi's feet on the floor and helped her climb the ladder to the top of the water tank.

The city looked romantic from the top, and the breeze simply added flavour to the enchantment. Shruthi glanced at me and blushed.

I smiled. I held her hand and got on my knees. Shruthi's heart began to pound. She knew exactly what I was going to say. She could not keep her exhilaration under control. She just held her breath and waited for those three lovely words that she had been longing to hear for more than a year.

I put my hand in my pocket and took out a marker. Shruthi glanced at the marker and appeared confused. I opened the marker and drew a thin ring around her long, neatly-shaped ring finger.

Shruthi gasped. I looked right into her eyes. "I wish I could take you right up to the clouds. But this is the closest I could manage. I may not have the money to buy you a solitaire ring at the moment. I may not be able to shower you with gifts. But what I can promise you is a heart brimming with immense love and a shoulder you can rest on for the rest of your life. WILL YOU MARRY ME?"

The words shot through Shruthi. She expected three words, but she got four instead. Her eyes welled up with happiness. Tears rolled down her soft cheeks.

"Yes," she nodded. "Of course, Abi. Let's get married right now."

I stood up and pulled her into me. I hugged her tight. The breeze blew her hair over her face. I gently guided her hair towards the back of her ear and kissed her forehead.

"I love you, Shruthi," I said.

"I love you too, Abi."

"Now let's get out of here before anyone catches us," I said.

"No. I want to stand here and hug you for some more time."

I smiled and kissed her on her forehead again. Shruthi wrapped her arms around me, and I wrapped mine around her.

• • •

The days that followed were days of congenial bliss. It had been a couple of months since we exchanged hearts and our romance blossomed into a cherubic flower that spread its enchanting fragrance all over the place. Although we were in different colleges, we made sure we met each other every day even if it was for a very short time.

Our short meetings during the day and long phone chats at night were carefully cherished. Slowly, she burrowed her way deeper and deeper into my heart and vice versa.

We learned a lot about each other in our 1440 hours of togetherness. I came to know that her family had moved down from the US when she was in sixth grade after her father's business went topsy-turvy. He partnered with his friend and started a garment export business in Chennai that had started to grow huge.

She had lost her mother, who had fallen victim to cancer, a year after they came to India. She had been looked after by her dad and her grandmother ever since.

She was a hardcore animal lover, who wouldn't mind giving shelter to stray cats and dogs once in a while. She had this crazy affinity towards cats and was often found running behind a random stray kitten.

Shruthi had a charming and impressive OCD habit when it came to dressing. She made sure that her finger and toe nails were painted with colours that either matched or complemented the colour of her clothes.

If clothes were living things and had the power to dream, they would have all dreamed of being a part of her wardrobe, as any attire would sit flawlessly on her exquisitely-shaped body. She was always keen that her hairstyle matched the type of clothes she wore and she had innumerable hair clips, ribbons and other hair accessories.

She was very understanding about my passion for cinema. She enjoyed writing and also loved watching movies with me. She was clearly aware of my growing family responsibilities and always stood by me, guiding me to make practical decisions when ever there was a glitch.

Abi, I am not going to college today. Can u take leave too? Dad n grandmom are not at home. They're off to Tirupur. There seems to be some issue with his business. I wanna meet u. Can u come home?

I skimmed through the text message on my mobile phone with half-open eyes, still lying under my blanket. My lips stretched wider as my brain comprehended what I was reading.

Sure baby. I'll be there in a couple of hours. I quickly realised that I had to inform Chalu, who would be waiting for me in his post-honeymoon attire.

Macha. I am not coming today. Going to meet Shruthi at her house.

Oh!

'Oh' was an instantaneous multi-purpose filler word that Chalu used whenever he did not know what to answer. In this context, he would have probably been waiting for me to pick him up and the sudden change in plan should have surprised him.

Another way of deciphering it was by assuming Chalu was excited about the idea that I was going to meet Shruthi in her house. It was all up to the people around him to elucidate the hidden meaning behind the'oh'.

You'd better come. If you know what I mean.;);P

Jokes apart. Have fun.

BTW, I have your helmet.

I read the series of messages sent by Chalu, as I gobbled up a few idlis without chutney or sambhar.

I know exactly what you mean. Perv. Keep the helmet. I will take it tomorrow.

"Aren't you going to college?" My dad asked as he swirled his steel tumbler of hot black tea.

"Nope. I am going to meet a friend to discuss a short film project," I said, without looking at his face.

My dad frowned.

"Bye," I shouted and ran out of the door ignoring my dad's eyebrows.

"Where is he going?" my mom asked her husband, completely unaware of the 'short' short film conversation he had with me.

"He's going to meet a girl. His girlfriend, maybe," he said with a wide grin.

• • •

I found myself ringing Shruthi's door-bell in less than a couple of hours with flowers for my darling.

I was dressed in a loose black shirt with the first two buttons left open, revealing my chest and a black beaded chain that Shruthi had gifted me. I wore dark blue jeans and dark grey shoes that blended well with my shirt. My hair was all messed up as a result of a dusty bike ride without a helmet.

Shruthi answered the door with her mobile phone to her ear.

"I'll call you back," she said and hung up.

She was dressed in a cute pink T-shirt and a long white skirt that had a slit below the knee on one side. A pink pony scarf held her hair into a long silky ponytail.

"Who was on the phone?" I whispered to Shruthi, with anxiety.

"Vineeth. Dad's business partner's son. He left his helmet here when he came last time."

"Oh," I replied still standing outside, half realising that Chalu's answers were becoming contagious.

"Why is your hair messed up?" she asked.

"It was going to get messed up anyway," I said with a wink and handed over the flowers to her.

"*Ahan.* You shouldn't have dressed up either," she quipped with a blush. "Thanks for the flowers. But should I let you in?"

Her eyes suddenly turned into a magnet that shot an opposite pole right into me.

I forced myself inside and pressed my lips to hers gently caressing her back.

"Abbbi. Not yet. My grandmom's here," she said, pushing me away.

"Holy crap! Why didn't you warn me?" I whispered with a terrified look on my face.

"Because she actually isn't here. Look at your face." She chuckled.

"Shruthi... I'm going to..." I tried to hold her.

She slipped away and ran into the bedroom screaming at the top of her voice. I chased her and caught her by the hip. I hugged her from behind and softly kissed the back of her neck.

Shruthi closed her eyes, held my head and gasped.

"I love you, Abi," she said.

"I love you," I said.

She turned around and looked me in the eyes. Her fingers drew a few circles on my bare chest and then slowly moved upwards and caressed my lips. She pressed her body against mine and kissed me deeply. I held her hip and guided my fingers along the length of her spine sending waves of chills through her. She held my shirt and pushed me on the bed falling on me.

"Are we going to have sex?" I asked, gasping for breath as Shruthi broke the kissing spree.

"I don't know. Let's just make out and see where this leads us to," she said and kissed me again.

• • •

10

A Promise to Myself

I wasn't making it in the real world. Just as I was wondering where my passion was leading me to, I received a phone call.

"What? Really? Are you sure?" I was hyperventilating over the call.

It was Jairam, the production manager I had met during the audition, a year ago. Although I had let Suresh Lal move on to pull out someone else's kidney, I was in constant touch with Jairam. He had always been nice and also referred me to a few of his contacts.

"Yes, Abhishek. I am producing a film. You will be playing a significant character in it," he said.

I did not get carried away by the news although my oxygen intake was high. I had automatically learned to control my excitement post my past experiences.

"Are you going to ask me for money?" I asked, trying to be very straightforward.

"No. Definitely not. I know how passionate you are. There are no strings attached. It was the producer and the director who master-planned the audition fee last time. They were never going to make a movie. It was all for money. I got to know about that very late, and I am extremely sorry about it."

"No problem, sir. I realised it late too," I said.

"Well, the good news is that our project is to kick off soon. We are going to have a *pooja* followed by a month-long shoot schedule to start with. Get to Coimbatore and call me," he said.

I suddenly felt like I had seen water trickling into the hole after digging the earth single-handedly for a real long time.

I reached Coimbatore and booked a lodge for a couple of hours, as Jairam said he was busy and he would meet me personally and take me to the place where accommodation was arranged.

As promised, Jairam met me in exactly two hours, and then he narrated the story to me, explained my character and also took my pictures to add in the print materials of the pooja. I accompanied him to the graphic designer's and was completely pumped to see my pictures on the posters and invitations.

"Okay. We are almost done. Let's go get some lunch," he said.

I was glad he uttered the word 'lunch' because I was starving. I hadn't had breakfast.

"Sure, sir," I said.

We were walking down the street to grab some lunch and get a few other things done after that, when it suddenly struck Jairam that he had forgotten his wallet at home.

"I am really sorry to ask you this, Abhishek. Can you lend me three thousand rupees? I will return it to you as soon as I get home," he said.

I had exactly three thousand rupees in my wallet. Had he checked my wallet or was it mere coincidence? Although I wasn't too keen on giving him the money, I decided to believe him. I gave him two thousand and five hundred rupees, keeping aside five hundred just in case of an emergency.

Jairam immediately took an auto rickshaw and extended to me an impromptu invitation to his house for lunch. On the way, he stopped at a liquor shop and treated himself to some alcohol, using the money I gave him. We pulled over at about four other liquor shops on our way, like a public transport bus stopping at appropriate locations.

By the time we reached his house, he had used up some of my money and all the balance on my phone to talk to random people, and he was so drunk that he probably didn't remember who I was.

I really wanted to get back to my room and wait until the next day as the *pooja* was to happen the next day. I happened to meet two of Jairam's friends at his house, who offered to drop me to my room. But I soon realised that my kismet had other plans for me when the two barflies directed their bikes to a local bar, where they authoritatively used up whatever was left in my wallet.

As the spirits intoxicated their medulla oblongatas, they decided to strike a deal with me. One of the two men claimed that he was the director Shankar's associate and that he was going to make a movie with Trisha as the heroine. He told me that he would make me the lead opposite her if I paid the production house ten lakhs.

"How do you like this deal?" he asked.

My experience had taught me to believe that every word he said was a lie.

"Can you please drop me to my room?" I said.

My response made the two of them sober. They wanted to fill their stomachs with more alcohol. I wished them "bon appétit" and walked back to my room, which was a good two kilometres away.

At the lodge, the receptionist asked for extra money to spend the night, and when he learned that I did not have any, he demanded to keep my phone until the next day, as I had promised him I would pay up the following day. The long walk had made me tired and hungry. I called it a night after feasting on a couple of biscuits that I had left from my travel to Coimbatore.

Jairam came to my room early the next day and gave me an apology from the bundle of excuses he carried on his hunchback, which he used to sanctify himself. I got introduced to another loser who proudly announced himself as the hero of the film.

Jairam had apparently been struck with memory loss again, as his wallet was still at home. I wondered if he even had a wallet.

He borrowed money from our hero and paid the room rent, getting my phone back in the process. He behaved as if he had just rescued me from being pulled into quicksand, oblivious of the fact that he had stripped someone else's clothes off in trying to do that.

But, ultimately what was gladdening was that we were heading for the pooja and the shoot would commence the following day.

On our way to the pooja location, my heart slapped me hard when the taxi slowly pulled over at a liquor shop. However, I was happy when I learned that the unit vehicle from Chennai was on its way and Jairam had pulled over so that they could catch up with us.

After about thirty minutes of waiting, with a flurry of phone calls, Jairam declared that the director of the film had suddenly bailed from the project. The news led him and our hero into the liquor shop, while the taxi was sent off, leading me to become an unbelievable basket case.

They came out in exactly thirteen minutes. Although they had spirits running through their brains, they had a neat solution to the apparent glitch we were in. Jairam proclaimed the hero as the director, while I had already started thinking of a way to get the next bus back to Chennai.

Now that the movie had a new director, Jairam was in the mood to celebrate.

The level of their intoxication began to badger the level of the auto driver's tolerance. He pulled his brakes midway and asked us to pay up and get out of the rickshaw.

This unanticipated act by the driver unveiled a small twist in the tale. Both the 'new director' and Jairam appeared rupee-less due to their alcoholic philanthropy. He snatched my mobile phone and attempted to exchange it for money at a nearby mobile store.

"Sir, you can't do that," I said and tried to snatch my mobile back.

"Abhishek. I will buy you a new phone later," he said, his tongue slipping through the words.

After a brief argument, he tossed the mobile back to me and asked me to wait with the auto driver, assuring him that he would be back with the money.

He returned after an hour, paid the auto fare and hired a taxi that was to finally take us to the *pooja* location, where at least a hundred people were waiting. However, my plight did not end there. We were to pick someone up on the way. Jairam asked me to get off and wait for that 'someone,' telling me that he would be back in ten minutes, as he had a small errand to run nearby. It took me an hour to realise that neither 'someone' nor Jairam was going to show up.

I was left abandoned on the street with absolutely no balance on my mobile phone and with bankruptcy echoing through the walls of my wallet. I took a bus to the lodge room with the little change that I carried and called my friend using the phone there, asking him to send me some money.

He said he would be able to make it only by late evening, which meant that I was to spend some more time in the lodge with a stomach that had not seen food since the previous day and with a head full of frustration and regret.

While I rested on my bed waiting for help, Jairam and the 'new director' came to my room. They were so drunk that they crashed onto the floor the moment they stepped in. I was so weary and stymied that I did not want to turn and look at them. Just when I convinced myself that my situation could not get worse, I noticed Jairam sitting beside me.

He placed his hand on my stomach. “Are you hungry?” he asked.

“Take your hands off me?” I said.

He moved closer and put his arms around me. He held my head and brought his head closer to mine, attempting to kiss me.

Now, this was my limit. I pushed him aside, picked up my bag and made a quick exit to the reception, telling them that I wanted to check out immediately. However, at the reception, I was told that I could not check out without removing the two inebriated occupants.

I explained my situation to them, to which they reciprocated well. They sent in a couple of well-built staff, who neatly towed them out and placed them on the road, where they were open to spending the rest of their night.

My friend came in the meantime and helped me get the next bus back home, carrying a whole lot of food and some bitter memories that were to lamentably linger in my head forever.

• • •

I reached home, walked straight into my room and slammed the door shut. I was thoroughly ashamed of myself. I was ashamed that I could not identify the right people in the industry. I was mortified that I couldn't see past my passion and I let people take advantage of it. I was dejected that I could not find the kind of break I wanted. I glanced at my mirror. I was downcast. I had tears in my eyes.

“I will not fall into these traps again,” I promised myself. If Shruthi was around I would have told her everything. She would have made me feel better. I wished Chalu and Peri were in Chennai. But they were all away sculpting their own lives. I did not want to talk to anyone else about it. Not even *Amma*, because she would start worrying about me.

I felt lonely. But I was confident that I would bounce back. I needed time for the wound to heal.

• • •

11

When Wounds Did Not Matter

I was seated in our classroom trying to listen to a boring lecture from Ilamparithi sir.

The classroom was well-ventilated with windows on all sides for the sunlight to trickle through plentifully.

There were twice the number of benches than the actual strength of the class, which we used for post-lunch nap breaks.

I couldn't get my mind off the skin-sharing affair I had experienced with Shruthi the previous day. The lecture echoed obscurely within my eardrums, and the waves of sound just did not touch my brain, no matter how much I tried. I looked around to see what my fellow classmates were up to and realised that I had active partners in crime, who were as inactive as I was.

Balasaravanan - busy texting his latest sincere love

Nithin – peeking into Bala's phone

Gautham – staring outside the window

Perinbanathan – playing the snake game on his overused Nokia 1100

Gayathri – sleeping

Krithika – licking through the remains of her Dairy Milk

Sreedev – sketching a holiday location

Renjith – writing something seriously (must have been a letter to the CM to legalise plagiarism)

Jaison and Manjunath – playing book cricket

Prabakaran and Harish – discussing the future of Indian cinema

Muruganandham – clicking candid pictures of Krithika attacking Dairy Milk

Vivek – carving his lover's name on his desk with a pen knife

Shiva – blowing the wood dust off Vivek's art

Chalukyan – he was just missing

My eyes wandered through the classroom in a sluggish attempt to spot Chalu. My joblessness was interrupted with a sharp vibration in my pocket caused by a text message as a result of someone else's joblessness. It was an SMS from Shruthi.

Shruthi: *I just rode past your college gate. I noticed Chalu arguing with a few guys outside. Is everything okay?*

Abi: *I'm not sure. He is not in class. Shall check.*

Shruthi: *Okay. Hey, u better bring Vineeth's helmet when u come in the evening. He might get pissed off if he knows I gave it to u.*

Abi: *Aarrghh! I told u I dint want it.*

Shruthi: *Protect to avoid regrets. Not only your head, also when on bed.;);););)*

Abi: *Point noted. :)*

Shruthi: *Good. Stay pointed.;)*

Abi: *Shut up. :D :). Class over. I'm gonna check on Chalu. Msg you later. Luv you.*

Shruthi: *Okay. See you in the evening. Love you too.*

I slid my phone back into my pocket as Ilamparithi sir delivered the final few words of his lecture.

"Thank you, Ananth, for paying attention. And for the others who did not even bother to pretend, you can always come and see me in case of doubts."

He smiled and walked out of the classroom carrying his thick book on television production as the lunch bell rang in the background, with seventeen grumbling stomachs chorusing in the foreground.

Just as I made the difficult decision of leaving my lunch box behind, in an attempt to go look for Chalu, he walked in wearing a confusing smile on his face.

"Where in the world were you?" I barked.

"Ummm... I was just hanging around," Chalu said, his smile completely out of sync with his attempted casual reply.

"Were you involved in an argument again?"

Chalu's smile escaped from his lips, realising he was caught red-handed. His eyeballs made necessary adjustments as he burnt the fat in his nimble mind thinking of a quick answer.

"Ahhh, never mind," he mumbled as he could not construct a suitable answer.

I stared at him, demanding some clarity for his peculiar behaviour. Chalu read my mind and smiled again making the situation even more obscure.

"I-I'll talk to you about it. Let's get something to eat first," he said and walked over to his seat.

The word 'eat' reminded me of my hunger. I took out my lunch box and opened it only to find nothing in it except a few full pieces of round black pepper.

Chalu simpered at me as I glanced at him.

"I don't like pepper in pongal. But the sambhar was yummy. Want some curd rice?" Chalu said, as he casually gobbled a few spoonfuls from his own lunch box.

"What the hell is wrong with you? Why are you behaving as though someone whacked your head with a hammer?" I shot at him, snatching his lunch and filling my mouth with Chalu's mom's special curd rice, which was garnished with grapes and pomegranate.

Chalu chewed his food and gestured, asking me to wait until he swallowed it. But before he did, we had a few visitors breaking into our classroom with gritted teeth and clenched fists. It was Jaffer, Susheel and Vimal, local lads from the B.Com department.

"Where is Chalukyan?" Susheel shouted at the top of his voice.

Peri, Harish and I sprung out of our seats and landed in front of them to avoid a scuffle as we were clearly aware of the physical damage these guys were capable of. Chalu had already gotten into an argument with them a few months earlier when he accidentally collided with Susheel and refused to apologise.

Susheel felt the act was insulting because he was with a junior girl.

Now that the damage was done, the team was waiting for an opportunity to pounce on him. Although his modus operandi was that of a goon, Susheel wanted to be a policeman. He always thought that the only way to earn respect was to instil fear in the people around him.

Jaffer and Vimal did not have any ambition. They just liked sticking together and making life miserable for everyone who messed with them.

"What's the matter, Susheel?" Peri interrupted.

"I am not here to talk to you." He pushed Peri aside and walked towards Chalu. "Come outside. We need to talk."

Chalu leaned back on his bench and glanced at him in the eye, skillfully hiding his fear.

"I'm hungry. Let me finish my lunch." He responded in a casual tone and continued to eat.

He made sure he picked only a morsel of rice at a time and took his own sweet time to chew it.

Jaffer got furious with Chalu's behaviour and stepped forward to hit him. Harish moved in swiftly, held his hand and nudged him away.

"You might want to think twice before attempting such foolishness again," he warned, "Now, why are you guys creating a scene? Is it that collision incident? Or is it because he said he will slit each one of your throats?"

I begged Harish with my eyes, asking him not to dig up the past.

"What? Did he say that?" Vimal asked.

Peri and I placed our hands on our heads realising Harish had just dabbed some aftershave on their burns.

"Vimal, he really does not know what he is talking about." I intervened. "What is the issue now? I'll come out with you. Let's talk this out."

"Yes. We've got to put an end to this. Mujahid *anna* wants to talk to him. Ask him to come outside," Vimal said.

"Chalu will come after his lunch. Let me talk to him meanwhile," I said and beckoned for Peri and Harish to join me.

• • •

We walked outside the college gate along with Susheel, Jaffer and Vimal, rolling up our shirt sleeves, in a determined mindset to talk the entire issue out. We noticed Mujahid at a distance, dropping an exhausted cigarette butt after having burned all the tobacco from it into his lungs.

Mujahid was the brother of a local politician and most evidently the leader of this pack of goons. Susheel, Vimal and the other sidekicks kept their voices at a high decibel knowing very well that Mujahid would be around to help keep their vocal chords active.

He stood by an old motor room, a few hundred yards away along with the other boys. The motor room was used as a hangout spot for the students, mostly as a smoking place and of course to solve issues between seniors and juniors. Some issues were resolved easily while the others climaxed only after some serious tugging, pulling and manhandling.

Harish, Peri and I headed towards the old motor room in an attempt to solve yet another issue. When we focused our eyes on the guys who stood with Mujahid, we realised that they weren't students but a few local hooligans, who looked like they had just gotten out of jail.

I quickly counted the number of people. There were at least thirty of them. Our eyeballs popped out. We knew very well that Mujahid and team were in no mood to talk the issue out. They were in the mood to pounce all over Chalu.

"Send a message to Chalu asking him not to come out whatsoever," I whispered to Peri who slowly took out his mobile and skillfully typed the message without even looking at his phone.

"Hi, *anna*. What's the problem?" Harish asked as we neared him.

"Where is Chalu?" Mujahid asked, straining his head and taking a look over our shoulders to check if he was hiding behind us.

"He is counting the rice grains in his lunch box," Susheel shot back before anyone else could answer.

I gave Susheel a cold glare.

"Who are you glaring at? Do you want to see yourselves fucked?" Vimal said in a tone that attempted to convey that he was a casual rowdy.

Harish tried to hold back his laugh, but it somehow escaped from his nose, making him snort.

Mujahid became furious.

"Do you think this is funny?" Mujahid barked, taking a few rapid steps forward, raising his hands to hit Harish.

"Whoa... whoa... whoa! *Anna*! Let's take it easy," I intervened. "I know it wouldn't take a minute for you to break his nose. But it goes vice versa too."

"How can you ever talk to *anna* that way?" Jaffer snarled, jumping in front of me and holding my collar.

Peri kept his hand on Jaffer's chest and attempted to shove him away.

"*Otha*. Bitch. You wag your tail and lift it up to whichever bastard you want. You can't expect everyone to do it," he said, his Tamil turning more local than usual.

The moment he said that, Mujahid's local jail breakers pounced on the three of us and held us against the wall of the motor room.

"You guys are so finished." Mujahid hissed. "Who wants to hit them first?"

A few of them raised their hands, out of which, he picked a boy who looked like he had just run away from primary school.

We pushed and pulled in between the hands of the locals. Harish leaned forward and grabbed the fingers of the guy holding him, with his teeth, putting his 'Dabur red' coated teeth to good use. The guy used his other hand and caught Harish's throat holding him tighter against the wall.

Just as the school-going Complan boy stepped forward clenching his calcium-rich fist, a jeep screeched to a halt right in the midst of the action scene. Every head turned uniformly towards the jeep, which had the word POLICE written on top of it.

The nimble-minded literates took to their feet and scattered in different directions shouting the word 'police,' in a frantic attempt to warn the other illiterates.

Jaffer, Mujahid, Susheel and Vimal quickly took their bikes and scooted away, without even lifting their side stands, as though they were in a hurry to hit the toilet as a result of some bad lunch.

Peri, Harish and I did not move an inch. We kept our eyes, which had grown bigger in size, on the jeep as we knew that we had just jumped from the frying pan into the fire.

I was expecting a warning and some advice from the police officers, while Harish and Peri worked their minds up to being rusticated and serving a jail term.

The doors of the police jeep opened and out came Edwin uncle and Chalu's father.

Edwin uncle was a sub-inspector and Chalu's family friend. He was tall, well-built and looked extremely young for his age. He stepped out of the jeep, dressed in his neatly pressed police uniform. He waved at me.

"Uncle! How did you get here?" I asked, relieved that we were in the safe zone.

Edwin uncle pointed at the college gate, where we found Chalu waving and walking towards us with a triumphant grin on his face.

We did not mind being a little filmy. We imagined him walking towards us in slow motion as he had not only saved us from swollen faces but also got us out of a possible suspension from college.

"I knew very well that these guys weren't going to settle for a talk. That is why I asked uncle to come," Chalu said.

"Why are you guys getting involved in unwanted fights?" Chalu's father asked. "These guys are goons. They are capable of anything."

"*Appa*, I told these guys not to go out. They did not listen to me," Chalu said.

We glared at Chalu but decided not to tell his dad anything about the whole scenario, just because he rescued us from being beaten black and blue.

"Alright. You guys head to class. We are going to have a word with the principal," Chalu's father said.

"What the hell did you do? Why were they all mad at you?" I asked Chalu, after making sure his dad and his friend were a good distance away from us.

"We got into an argument. I threatened them that I would walk into their department and break their noses," Chalu said.

"Wha... why? You know very well that these guys are a bunch of immature losers. Why do you even have to go talk to them?" I said.

"I did not get into an argument for the sake of arguing," Chalu shot back. "Shruthi drove past this way, and these guys passed some bad comments about her. I don't think she heard it. But I did not like it."

"You should have broken their noses right there," I fumed.

"Why are you fuming? They are a bunch of immature losers. Aren't they?"

I smiled.

"I'm sorry, *macha*," I said.

"It's okay. Now that you are less angry, I would like to tell you one more thing."

I glanced at Peri and Harish, who frowned as much as I did.

"They did pass comments about Shruthi. But that is not the only reason why I fought with them."

Our frowns grew stronger. Chalu took a few steps away from us. "Poornima was passing this way too. I was trying to find a way to grab her attention, and this opportunity came up. But look on the brighter side. I managed to break two windows with just one stone."

Chalu sprinted towards the college gate as soon as he said that. Peri, Harish and I exchanged irritated looks and realised that we had to chase him down and show him our muscle power.

"Dog! You almost got our teeth removed just because you wanted to get someone's attention?" I yelled as I chased him.

Chalu ran through the open gate and scurried towards our department as we followed him. Just as he entered the department, he bumped into someone and fell on the floor. He stood up to find Renjith standing in front of him with tears in his eyes. He had a piece of paper in his hand and appeared to be extremely tense about something.

"Dude! Are you okay? Is there a problem?" Chalu asked, as we caught up with him, panting heavily. Renjith handed him the piece of paper, which was untidily folded into four.

We put our heads together as Chalu unfolded it. It was a letter.

"Renji,

Dad came to know about our relationship. He is extremely furious. We had a huge argument. Being my father, an MLA and a last word freak, he obviously had to win it hands down. The result? A few thrashings and house arrest. I don't think I will come to college anymore. My dad's planning to send me off to Coimbatore this Saturday and get me married in a month's time.

I don't want to go. I know this is too early to ask. But, shall I come to you? Can we get married? I am scared, Renji. I don't want to lose you. Please reply at the earliest.

Love you so much, Jesse"

The boys were shell-shocked. They glanced at Renjith, who appeared to be completely broken down.

"Who brought you this letter?" I asked.

"Fincy. Jesse's friend."

"Do you think we should go talk to her dad?" Chalu said.

"No *da*. The man is very adamant. He will not settle for anything."

"What have you decided?" Peri asked, softly.

"I am going to discontinue my studies and elope. I have no other choice."

"Dude, we just have a couple of months to finish our course," Harish said.

"I know. But I only have a couple of days to save the love of my life. I can't let this go at any cost. I have made my decision. I will call you guys once we are out of here and safe."

"Excuse me. Do you realise that you have friends to help you elope?" I said.

"No *da*. I don't want you guys to get involved with this mess. Her dad's quite capable of anything. Let me take care of this myself."

"Send word to Jesse that you will come for her on Saturday. Guys, we have a little planning to do," I said, pretending to be deaf to Renjith's words.

• • •

"I will miss you guys. I'll call you as soon as I get to Bangalore." Renjith was amid the Wizguys. We had all gathered to send him off at the airport. As per my plan, he was to go to Bangalore and wait for Jesse, who would promptly be picked up from her train to Coimbatore and dropped at the airport to take the next flight to Bangalore. I asked Renjith to leave early as I thought it would be safer that way.

"I will wait for Jesse at the Bangalore airport. Please be careful, guys. I owe you guys a ton."

Nithin's eyes welled up. He stepped forward and hugged him.

"I'll miss you, buddy."

"Wait, this is getting too emotional. Let's part in style," Renjith said and held his palm up gesturing for all of us to place our hands on his, one above the other.

Eighteen hands were piled up within a matter of seconds.

"WIZGUYS, TONIGHT WE DINE IN HELL."

Renjith shouted at the top of his voice.

All of us laughed not caring one bit about the stares we received from the people around us.

"Let's not get sentimental, guys. We will be in touch. Love you all. Keep me posted on what's happening." Renjith turned around and swiftly walked towards the security, who was checking ID cards and letting people into the airport terminal. I knew he was in tears.

"Okay. Let's go, guys. We have a train and a flight to catch," I said.

• • •

Jesse walked into the Central railway station with her father's gang members, who were all dressed in white shirts and *dhotis*. Jesse was dressed in a yellow kurta and black jeans as instructed by me.

Nithin, Chalu and Vivek glanced at her from a distance. Vivek was dressed in the same clothes as Jesse, and with his long hair wig he looked exactly like her body double. Jesse and her *dhoti*-clad companions boarded the Coimbatore Express that was waiting in platform number four.

Nithin nudged his friends to move forward, behaving as though he was carrying cocaine in his shirt pocket and a couple of sticks of dynamite in his pants. They nervously boarded the train and stood by the toilets. Nithin tried his best to act casual, but his over-expressive eyes threatened to invite trouble.

The long horn of the train was heard. Nithin related the horn to the sound of conch shells blown at funerals. His hands started shaking. Just as the train began to move, Jesse rose nervously from her seat and walked towards the toilet, dropping her mobile phone on the floor as she stood up.

"Where are you going?" one of her dad's dogs asked.

Jesse pointed at the toilet and continued to walk without saying a word.

Vivek turned around and faced the toilet, with his back to her dad's men.

As Jesse neared the toilet, Nithin and Chalu put a shawl around her and dragged her out of the train.

Back inside the train, the men in white kept an eye each on Vivek (disguised as Jesse), who pretended to be waiting to use the toilet.

Soon after the train picked up speed, Vivek sprinted through a couple of compartments and entered a toilet before being noticed. He removed his kurta and slipped into a casual blue shirt. He pulled out his wig and flung it outside the train through the little window in the toilet.

He walked out of the toilet, straight into the *dhoti*-clad men, who, by now, had already realized that Jesse was missing and had started looking for her. Vivek casually sat down in the seat that was booked for him according to the plan.

• • •

"Hello. I can't hear you. Speak louder," Chalu shouted into his phone, which was placed between his ear and his helmet.

He was on his bike with Jesse on the way to the airport.

"Looks like Jesse's people have a fair idea of where she is now. They found her phone in the train. They are reading Renjith's text messages," Vivek said, trying to keep his voice loud enough for Chalu and low enough so that he wasn't overheard by the hyperventilating hooligans.

"I'll take care of it. Over and out," Chalu said and accelerated. Jesse clenched her teeth and held on tight. The speedometer needle threatened to jump out of the moving bike and commit suicide.

Chalu's bike screeched to a halt at the airport entrance, where Peri and I were waiting.

"Dude. Get going. They've found Jesse's mobile. They'll be here any minute," Chalu said.

"Haha. I asked Jesse to drop the mobile on purpose," I said, with a wink. "I sent her a text message from Renjith's number with an entirely different escape plan. They will be looking for her at the Koyambedu bus stand now."

"That's awesome," Peri said.

"Okay Jesse. Let's go. You have a marriage to attend," I said.

Just as we started to leave, I noticed something in the distance. I squinted my eyes trying to focus on what caught my eye.

"Guys, accompany Jesse to the terminal. I've got some work to do," I said and rushed away from the question marks on top of my friends' heads.

• • •

I stood nervously in front of Shruthi's house, waiting for someone to answer the door. I had many things running through my mind. Would her dad doubt me? How would her grandmother react? Who would open the door? What do I tell them as soon as they find me in front of them?

No, I wasn't going to ask for Shruthi's hand. Not yet. But I had to do this. It was her birthday. I wanted to surprise her. I checked my watch. It was 11:58 PM. I had actually planned to jump over the wall and sneak in through her balcony. But realising the consequences it would gather if I was caught, I decided to do it the harder way.

The door opened, revealing her dad, dressed in loose nightwear, yawning at my face with sleepy eyes. Her dad looked smart for a 50-year-old. He was bald, with a grey French beard. There were a few tiny wrinkles on his fair, round face.

"Yes. May I help you?" he said, as I ran my eyes over my future father-in-law.

"Ummm. H-Hello, Uncle. I-I am Shruthi's friend. It's her birthday in..." I paused to look at my watch. "... two minutes. I just wanted to give her a surprise."

He scanned me from head to toe like the security staff at the airport check-in counter. I was obviously dressed well. I wore a yellow V-neck t-shirt and blue jeans. My beige sneakers matched the colour of the box I was carrying. There was a small plaster on my forehead, which he noticed and frowned at.

"I can explain that." I wanted to tell him.

"SHRUTHIII," he yelled.

I almost dropped the box that I held.

"You have a guest," he shouted.

The clock struck twelve.

I could hear the sound of her anklets running towards the door. They sounded curious. She got towards the door and halted. She was dressed in a pink T-shirt and loose yellow pyjamas. Her messy hair made it evident that she had sprung straight out of bed. She still looked adorable. I decided to take a moment to gaze at her while she decided which expression to fix on her face—surprise, fear or anger. She glanced at her dad, still not able to come up with a reaction.

Her dad forced a smile and put his arms around her. "Happy birthday," he said and swiftly walked inside.

Shruthi appeared relieved now. She did not expect her father to be cool about this unexpected surprise.

"Come in," she said.

"Come out," I said. "Now!"

"No way."

"Just by the lawn," I pleaded.

Shruthi closed the door behind her and walked out, tying her hair into a bun as she placed her bare feet on the cement floor of the small compound around her independent house. The floor was wet with the showers that had come in a few hours ago. The air was fresh and smelled of damp earth.

I held her hand and led her into the lawn. She squealed in delight as the wet grass tickled her feet. I lead her to a small lemon tree that stood right in the centre of the lawn. From the look on her face, I realised she was confused about what I was trying to do.

I held the branch of the tree and shook it. The water droplets that accumulated on the leaves showered on her head. Although it was a very clichéd romantic scene, she seemed to like it.

"Abbbiiiii," she squealed in a low decibel.

She held her arms wide apart as the water droplets kissed her. I wanted to hug her. A few lemons fell on my head warning me to behave. I opened the large box that I carried and asked her to put her hand inside and feel her gift.

"What is this? A soft toy?" she asked, running her fingers through the gift inside. "Wait... is this what I think it is?" she said, her eyes beaming with excitement.

She gently took it out. It was a lovely white kitten with four black paws.

"Meet Socks," I said.

"Awww. She is so cuuutteee."

"It's a he."

"I love him, Abi," she said, caressing his head and placing him back in the box.

"What about me?" I said, failing miserably to make a cute puppy face.

"I love you too, my baby." She gave me a little peck on my cheek. Maybe my puppy face was cute enough for her.

"Someone's in sparrow mode. Dealing in small pecks. Is that all you've got for a hungry boyfriend?"

"Kitchen closes at midnight." She winked.

"I like this clown dress," I said, pointing at her loose pyjamas.

"This is what you get when you show up when the world's asleep," she said, frowning.

"I want to kiss you now," I said.

"Can you explain that plaster on your forehead?" She changed the topic.

"This happened when I was on a little rescue mission."

"Can you elaborate?" She put her hand on her hip.

"On the day I was with Jesse in the airport, I found Socks stuck in a thorny bush. I had to ask my friends to see Jesse off so that I could go rescue him. He gave me this reward during my attempt."

She looked at me for a while. Her eyes sparkled in the compound light. There was a moment of silence.

"I think you deserve a hug." She leaned forward and hugged me after making sure there was no one spying on us.

I kissed her on her forehead and gently tapped her nose with my forefinger.

"I love you," I said.

"I love you too," she said. "Okay now, leave before my dad spots us making out on the lawn." She pushed me.

"I like the idea of making out on the lawn."

"You wish. Leave." Her eyeballs grew rounder and sterner.

I shook my head.

"Fine! I am going," she declared.

She picked up Socks' box and tiptoed out of the lawn.

"Shruthi," I called from behind.

She turned around, her hair falling loose from the bun in the process.

"Happy birthday."

"Thanks. Love you, hero," she whispered and blew me a kiss.

The marks on my forehead were completely worth it.

12

Hero's Friend

The marks created in Coimbatore continued to linger. I could somehow get over the bad treatment I underwent. But I just could not get my mind off being harassed sexually.

I continued to write scripts for cartoons, send my pictures to production companies and send numerous emails to Shruthi.

I soon became an old favourite for my relatives to gossip about. My parents decided to stop pestering me to look for a job. I could understand their frustration, but my passion kept whispering to me that I would make it someday.

"Abi," my dad called.

I was sitting in front of my mirror looking at myself for quite some time. It had been eighteen months since my last unsuccessful adventure in cinema.

I had acquired a few extra pounds. My face was not as fresh as it used to be. My hair receded by a line, displaying a larger forehead. I had absolutely nothing running in my head. After the Coimbatore incident, I began to assist a director for a year and a half.

We worked on a script for over a year and one fine day he happened to watch *Saw*, the English movie. The film apparently inspired him, urging him to shelf the script we were working on and begin with the adaptation of *Saw*. He had also promised me a role in the film.

We worked on the script for another six months until I realised that the director had no basic filmmaking sense. Not even as much as I knew. All he was good at was flapping his tongue endlessly and making people believe that he was aware of everything in the world. It took me eighteen months to learn that he was a talking toy parrot that could not fly. Better late than never, I bailed out of the project.

I glanced at my dad who stood by the door.

"Can we have a chat?" He asked.

"Oh yes. Why not?" I said.

He walked into my room and sat on my bed. We glanced at each other. I knew what he was going to talk about.

"How is it going Abi?" he asked.

"What?"

"Your quest for a career in cinema."

"I have a few prospects lined up. I've been following up with them," I said, without looking at his face.

My dad stared at me for a while.

"Can you just look back and count the amount of your time cinema has eaten up?"

I leaned back in my chair and roughly counted the number of years it had been since I graduated from college.

"Four-and-a-half years," I said, just realising that it was too long a wait. My dad nodded his head.

"Yes. Four-and-a-half years. Do you think you are doing justice to yourself and your family?"

"*Acha*, I've been managing the expenses at home right?" I said.

"It's not about making ends meet, Abi. It's about settling down in life. Your mom is worried about you. I am worried about you."

"But, I can't quit cinema just like that. It is a dream that I have been nurturing since childhood. You know that."

"I am not asking you to quit cinema. Get a job. Start working. Earn a regular income. Settle down. You can look for opportunities. That way you'll at least have a job to fall back on, just in case you trip.

You are getting old, son. In a few more years, companies may reject you for your age. You will be stranded. I have absolutely nothing to gain by asking you to work. My life is almost over. I want you to secure your life and save yourself from falling prey to this cinema dream.

I am aware of many families that are still suffering due to false hopes in cinema. The industry looks glossy and meritorious from the outside. But there is an unimaginable amount of suffering inside. People only know of the thousands who have succeeded. Millions have not.

You are educated. I am sure you would be sensible enough to understand. Act before it is too late. You are a hard worker, and I know how passionate you are. I am pretty sure you will get into movies some day. I am just asking you to look for an alternative means to support yourself until then."

I listened to him patiently. Every word he said made sense. I was a little too carried away in the beginning. But later, by the time I learned what the real world was, I had already fallen prey to it. From there it was more of an ego issue. My ego needed me to prove myself to all those who talked behind my back. That ended with me being in a lot more trouble. As dad said, I definitely had to make my foundation stronger. I had to find a job.

"Sure *acha*. I will think about it," I said.

"Good," he said and rose.

He caressed my hair and walked out of my room.

• • •

"I really don't know what to do, *da*. I have never thought of a career outside cinema," I told Rohit, my school mate.

I was at Rohit's house in Chennai. After my dad's advice, I began to think of finding a job seriously. But I had no clue where to start.

"What are your skill sets?" Rohit asked.

"Skill sets?"

"Yes. What do you think comes to you naturally other than acting?"

"Well, I've been doing some writing," I said.

"You can try and find a job as a content writer. Or ... wait ... you speak English. Do you want to try working in a call centre?" Rohit's eyes gleamed as though he just found the perfect career option for me.

"A call centre? Do you think I will fit in?" I asked, not too sure about how a call centre functioned.

"I guess you will. You speak good English. Plus you can act, which means you will have more spontaneity. You will be perfect for sales."

"Sales?" The word gave me shivers.

"Yes," he said.

"No way."

"Oh, come on. It's not as difficult as it sounds. My company is hiring voice support representatives now. You can apply."

"Oh, so you are campaigning for your company?" I said, trying to pull his leg.

"Shut up. I am trying to help you here. I think this is the best place to start with. I can try and rope you into the process in which I am a manager," he said.

"So, I will have to work under you?"

"Obviously. I am 'four years senior' to you," he said, holding his hands up to make air quotes. "I started as a customer service representative, got promoted to senior CSR to quality analyst to team leader to manager. It's been a long way up."

I took a good look at him for a moment. I just realised the value of lost time. While I was being knocked around from one hole to another like a golf ball, my friends were busy shaping their careers. I had absolutely no clue how to work in a corporate office. I thought it would be a good idea to work with Rohit, at least to start with so that I would have someone to go to whenever I needed some guidance.

"Okay. How do we do this?" I asked.

"Let's create a resume for you to start with. I will fix an interview for you. Once you are through, we will take it from there. What say?" he said.

It sounded neat. Now all I had to do was throw some of my details on a piece of paper. Since I had no experience, except for some bitter moments on the wrong side of cinema, it appeared more like a single page of personal information or a bio data. It took ten minutes for Rohit and me to work on my resume. He emailed it to his HR department and called one of his HR friends, asking her to fix an interview at the earliest.

"Your interview is on Tuesday in Bangalore," he said.

"That's like the day after tomorrow," I said.

"Yes. That's right. I am going to Bangalore tonight. You can come with me if you want."

"No *da*. I need time to pack."

"Cool. Then get a night bus tomorrow. You will reach early morning the next day. Get off at Madiwala. I will pick you up," he said.

"Okay *da*."

I couldn't believe things were happening so fast. Whether good or bad, I was going to take this up, at least to make my parents happy. I was never going to let go of cinema. This was just going to be a tiny break so I could bounce back with greater energy.

• • •

"Take a sweater or a jacket with you. Bangalore is cold at this time of the year," my dad said.

"I have already packed his sweater," my mom said.

"And I am taking my jacket too," I said.

My family was around me as though I was going to the USA and was never going to return.

"Abi, let me know if there are job openings in finance. I have to start looking for other options too, in case I don't get through campus placements," Veena said.

Oh yes. While my friends had gone ahead of me, my sister, who was four years younger, had caught up with me. She was doing an MBA in finance and had just a few more months left for graduation.

"Let me get placed here first. I have no clue how the interview is going to be," I said.

"Don't worry. Everything will fall in place," dad said.

It wouldn't. At least, not yet. To me, everything would have fallen into place only after I anchored my ship at the port of cinema. Until then, I was just going to sail like a harmless pirate, heading in the direction the wind took me.

"Okay folks. I am off. Wish me luck," I said.

"Good luck. Get to Bangalore and call me," mom said.

"Sure, bye," I said and walked out.

This was not the first time I was packing my bags and leaving home on the quest for a career. However, this time around I was travelling for a job outside cinema. I was travelling with certainty.

• • •

13

The First Time I Packed

I vroomed my Activa through the college gate ignoring the speed breaker at the entrance. Chalu clutched my shoulders, for one last time, happy that we finally got to college after a rough ride.

"Will you tell me why you are so excited?" he asked.

"Follow me," I said as I got off the bike after parking it in the college bike shed.

I ran into our department, Chalu trying to keep pace with me. I ran straight into the staff room and skidded to a halt before Ilamparithi sir's desk.

"Sir, they selected me," I said, not waiting for my breathing to settle down.

"What? Awesome. Way to go, Abi," Ilamparithi sir said. He grabbed both my hands and shook them excitedly.

Chalu came running in and spotted the handshake.

"What did I miss?" he asked.

"They selected me for acting in the TV serial I auditioned for."

"What???" Chalu could not believe it. "That's awesome." He ran and lifted me. Arun sir, Suresh sir and Gandhimathi ma'am gathered around to congratulate me.

"This is the first step towards your career, Abi. I am happy for you," Arun sir said.

"You have made us proud," Suresh sir said.

"Stay grounded. You have a long, long way to go," Gandhimathi ma'am said.

I had auditioned for the serial a couple of weeks ago. I wasn't really interested in soaps, but this one was a college story and was directed by a renowned person. It was produced by Pyramid Saimira, which was a reputed production company and I was offered a very important role. Moreover, it supposedly had a young couple in it. Solid reasons to accept the offer.

I heard voices shouting "TREAT" outside the staff room. The news had officially become public, thanks to Chalu. I already started making rough calculations on how much I would have to spend for the treat.

• • •

I took a close look in my mirror at home. I looked decent enough after the facial I did the previous day.

"Will you move away from the mirror? I am trying to do my hair here," Veena said.

"Don't you see I am busy?" I said.

She pushed me away and occupied the area in front of the mirror. I chuckled and went back to packing. I made sure I placed my best clothes in the huge bag I was going to take for the shoot.

"Abi, what time is your train?" mom asked.

"Four."

"Shall I make chapattis for dinner?"

"It is okay, *ma*, I'll buy food on the train," I said.

"Do you have money for your expenses?" dad asked.

"The production company will take care of that," I said.

"They may not cater to all your needs. Here, keep this."

My dad put two thousand bucks into my hand.

"Make sure you are confident in front of the camera. Don't be afraid," he said.

My dad had done small roles in a few Malayalam films. He had also produced a couple of movies, which were disasters at the box office. The wound that it created never healed causing him to lose his fondness for films.

"I can take care of this, *acha*. It's just a serial after all," I said.

"Good luck, Abi. Get me something from Coimbatore," Veena said.

"Yeah. Let's see."

I checked my watch. It was 2 p.m. I had to leave in an hour. I took a quick bath and packed up clothes, shoes, deodorant, hair brush, hair spray, cream and all that was necessary for the shoot. I took blessings from my parents and left for a ten-day journey that would kick-start my dream.

• • •

I got introduced to more than a dozen co-actors on my way to Coimbatore—Anand, Daniel, Roy, Tushaar, Nisha, Saranya, Ramya, Karthik, Mukesh, Ali, John, Manju, Kannan, Najum, Arya and many others.

It is going to take me a decade to memorise and match all those names to the right faces, I thought.

On the ten-hour long journey, I learned that the serial was going to be fresh and youthful and was to be aired on Vijay TV, which was one of the leading channels in Tamil.

Early next day, I found myself in a straight line along with the other actors. We were at a college in Coimbatore, where our shoot was to happen. The director, Ashish Bhaskar, was picking people at random for the initial sequence.

I took a good look at the director, about whom the entire train compartment was raving the previous night. He was fair, stout, plump and had a French beard. His voice sounded as though he had swallowed a whistle on his way to Coimbatore. He pointed his forefinger at eleven of us, three girls and eight guys, one after the other, and I heaved a huge sigh within when his finger pointed at me.

The others were told that they would get an opportunity in the next round and could work as junior artistes in this one. I did not know whether to be happy that he chose me or be sad that the others were not selected.

Why did they even call them if they were not going to be selected? I thought.

Everybody except Roy was a college student in real life. Roy was in his late thirties. He was tall, dark and well-built. Although he was smart, he looked older than his age. He took time to mingle with people and carried the 'I-am-a-senior-artist-respect-me' tag wherever he went.

Our very first shot was an action sequence — a conflict between the good guys and the bad guys. Roy was supposed to hold Tushaar's collar and deliver a few pre-written dialogues. I was asked to step in and ask Roy to take it easy.

We had three retakes for the entire scene because, each time I stepped in, I blocked someone else standing behind me.

"Blue shirt. Idiot," the director screamed through the mic.

Unfortunately, I was the only one who was wearing a blue shirt and I knew he had issues with my positioning.

"How many times will I tell you not to block the boy standing behind you? One more time you repeat the same mistake, I will replace you."

I started shaking. I suddenly lost confidence in myself. This was obviously the first time I was facing a big camera. In the two years I was in college, I had only acted in front of small handy cams handled by close buddies. I was so carried away with the appreciation and laurels in college that I could not accept being shouted at.

I was getting a trial run of the real world. Life in college was just a taste of what I was going to face on the outside. I knew I had to get used to it.

"Sorry, sir," I said and rehearsed my entry.

Fortunately, I managed to pull the shot off in the next take.

• • •

"Hello, hero. How was your first day?" Shruthi asked.

I was back in the hotel room after a nervous first day of shooting and was talking to Shruthi. I was distraught with my performance all day. I took numerous takes to deliver my dialogues, which caused a lot of uneasiness for the other actors.

"Not all that great," I said, pressing my phone against my ear as I made myself comfortable on the couch.

"Awwwwwww," she said.

"Why do you *awwww* all the time?" I asked, raising my voice.

"Why are you shouting?"

"Because I hate it," I said.

"What's wrong with you? Why are you acting crazy?" she asked in concern.

"Yes. I am crazy. I am an idiot. I am not what you thought I am. I am neither a good actor nor a good boyfriend. Bye."

I hung up before she could reply. I put my phone aside and stared at the ceiling.

Why did I get angry? I asked myself.

I replayed the conversation in my head. Was it because I couldn't get my expressions right at the shoot? Was it because I was humiliated in front of my co-actors? Was it because I suddenly felt I wasn't talented? Was it because I had just fallen from the topmost position of the card castle I had built within me?

Whatever it was, I shouldn't have raised my voice at her. She was the only medicine for my emotional state at the moment. I felt awfully sorry.

I quickly picked my phone and gave her a ring. She answered it immediately, as though she was waiting for my call.

"I'm sorry," I said.

"Awwwwww," she said.

I laughed.

"Tell me why you're upset," she said.

I narrated every frame my eyes and ears had captured that day. She listened to me patiently.

"You know, you have an ego," she said, softly.

"I do?"

"Yes. You haven't seen too much failure in life. You have been surrounded by praise and applause that you haven't tried to see through it. This is the real world, sweetheart."

May be she was right.

"And success stories are like Indian commercial cinema. You cannot narrate one without a fight sequence. Hard work, dedication and determination are your weapons here. You had a bad day today. Push it from your mind and pick yourself up. You can do it, baby."

"I love you Shruthi. You mean a lot to me," I said.

"Awwwww," she pushed one in again.

"I mean it. You laugh with me when I am happy. You pump me up when I am down. You are indeed my better half; a half that fits me so perfectly."

"You do that too, Abi. It's just that you don't realise it," she said.

"We are made for each other. Aren't we?" I said, dramatically.

She laughed.

"Talking about pairs. Did you meet your pair in the serial?"

"Nope. Not yet," I said, pretending to be disinterested.

"Don't pretend. I know you are excited to romance someone onscreen."

"Part of acting. Depends on what the script demands," I tried to be diplomatic.

"That's a safe answer." She chuckled.

We spoke for a couple of hours, and I felt much better. All the frustration and disappointment eased away. I would never have been able to find a better partner. Not even onscreen.

• • •

A few days after my first ever shot at the professional level, I learned that acting was not as easy as I had thought. I learned to be extra careful about what words I used on the sets because people were sensitive. I learned that the character I played was named Abi too. I learned that I would be acting with experienced actors like Swaminathan and Rajan P Dev. I learned that Saranya was to act as my partner. I learned that the director began to like my performance. I learned that there were a few people who were jealous of me and were waiting to pull me down.

"I really liked the way you glared at Roy in the last scene," Swapna, the lead actress told me during the shoot break.

"Thanks, *chechi*."

"But the guy really seems to be developing a dislike for you," she said.

"Yeah! I don't know why though," I said.

"Welcome to the industry," she said.

I smiled and glanced at the scene in the script I was reading. My next shot was a romantic line with my onscreen girlfriend, and I wanted to make sure I perfected it on the first take because doing a romance scene well was a matter of prestige for a guy of my age.

"Abi, Saranya. We are ready for the take," assistant director Muthu announced through the mike.

I handed over the script to another assistant director and walked towards the camera. Muthu came up to me and re-read my dialogues to me as I walked in.

"I am ready, *anna*," I said.

Saranya came into the frame. She appeared more confident than me. I smiled at her.

"Abi, I am nervous," she whispered to me.

"You don't look it. It's just a tiny dialogue. Let's *chemistrify* it," I said.

"*Chemistrify*? Is that even a word?"

"No. It's an emotion," I joked.

"Going for take," said the director.

"Ready, sir." We shouted in chorus.

"Roll. Camera. Action!!!"

Saranya: Abi, I heard you bought gifts for everyone for our trip to Ooty.

Me: Yes Devi.

Saranya: What have you got me?

I took out a sweater that had the words Abi and Devi separated by a heart symbol that was neatly knit on it.

Me: Take this. It's my sweater. My favourite.

Saranya: I love this, Abi. But what will you do without a sweater?

Me: I don't need one.

Saranya: Why?

Me: Because I have you.

Saranya: Shut up.

She blushed.

Me: I would keep my mouth shut for the rest of my life to see you blush.

"Cut," the director yelled.

The laughter bags that had been filling us up with each dialogue burst as soon as the director said cut.

"Abi. Awesome. Saranya. Super. You both make a great pair," he said.

I folded my hands and gestured for him to spare us from rumours. The director patted my back and smiled.

"Break," he shouted.

I wondered how he managed to produce so much sound with that compressed throat. My eyes focused on Roy, who looked at me from a distance. I smiled at him. He frowned and turned away.

• • •

The scene that followed was fun. It was an encounter between us and a few local goons in Palakkad headed by Rajan P Dev sir. People gathered around to watch the shoot as a result of the powerful tugging, pulling and shouting.

I appeared to be the most thrilled in the lot because I was one among the few Malayalis on the set, who knew that we were acting with a famous Malayalam cinema personality, who had acted in over two hundred movies. He was famous for his villainous roles but was an extremely down to earth and humorous person in reality.

He sat in an isolated area during the shot break, chewing betel leaves. I desperately wanted to go talk to him.

"Hi, sir," I said, nervously.

"Aah Abi. Come. Take a seat."

He dragged a chair towards him. I was glad he remembered my name.

"I am thrilled to share screen space with you, sir," I said.

He placed his hand on my shoulder.

"You must grow so much that someone else says this to you," he said.

I managed to strike a conversation with him. We spoke about his films like *Thommanum Makkalum* and *Pandippada.* He even enacted a few dialogues from the scene. He told me about how he got into movies from stage plays and his little experience in cinema. He also mentioned that he had an eyesight problem, which he was worried about.

A few localites gathered around us. They did nothing but stare at us, overhearing our conversation. A couple of them appeared drunk and carried with them a few bottles of toddy.

"Sir, would you like to have some toddy?" one of them asked.

"I am sorry, brother. I cannot entertain you during work hours," he joked.

Everybody laughed.

"Can I have your autograph?" he asked.

"Sure."

He looked around trying to find a pen and paper, his toddy influenced legs practising for *Nach Baliye* in the process. I offered him one.

Rajan sir signed and gave it to him.

"Take his autograph too. He is going to be a big star," he said, pointing at me.

Although I knew he said that because he did not want me to feel left out (I was not), I felt immensely happy to have heard those words from him.

After a round of hesitation and compulsion, I finally obliged to sign the paper. I glanced at Rajan sir and smiled.

"Thank you so much, sir. You made my day," I said.

"You are soon going to get used to this Abi."

I took his blessings and marched out of the area engraving the moment in my heart which would be cherished forever.

• • •

14

Signing Into Reality

"*Anna*, have we reached Madiwala yet?" I asked the bus conductor.

He shook his head.

"Okay. Where have we reached?"

He glanced up at me and spoke in Kannada. Now, was he swearing at me for annoying him for the third time at three in the morning?

"Koodhkolli," he said, after delivering a minute-long Kannada speech without subtitles.

I did not want to find a translator. From his actions, I learned that we had not reached Madiwala yet. I took my phone out and messaged Rohit.

"Dude, I have reached Koodhkolli. I should be there in some time," I messaged, as though I knew every bus stop in Bangalore.

"ROFL. Koodhkolli means 'sit'. It is not a bus stop," Rohit replied.

I ROSLed (rolled on my seat, laughing).

"Okay. Let's keep this joke between us," I texted, still unable to control my giggling.

• • •

I reached Madiwala an hour later. From the way the conductor looked at me, I really felt like he wanted to drag me and throw me out of the bus. As dad mentioned, Bangalore was cold. I put on my jacket. A large number of auto rickshaw drivers swarmed around me, wearing monkey caps and sweaters, each attempting to tow me into their vehicle.

I fought through the crowd and got to Rohit, who stood a few meters away, waiting for me with his bike. He placed my bag on his petrol tank and started the bike.

"Koodhkolli," he said and laughed.

"I thought we had a deal," I said.

"I was just asking you to sit," he said, still laughing.

I punched his back and sat on the bike. We reached his house in less than five minutes. He stayed in a paying guest accommodation in BTM. His room looked neat and cosy. It was meant for two people, with two beds, two work tables, a couple of chairs, a bean bag and an attached bathroom.

"You have a roommate?" I asked

"Had. He just shifted to Hyderabad. You can stay here. We'll share this room," he said.

"If I get the job, that is," I pointed out.

"You will. I have it all set up. All you have to do is show your face and speak a few words at the interview," he said.

"Okay *da*."

"Alright. Let me get some sleep. I am on night shift. You rest too. The interview is at 4 PM. We have a lot of time."

I glanced at the spare bed. It looked cosy and inviting. I needed to catch a few winks too, after a six-hour bus ride. I crashed on the bed before Rohit did and called it an extended night.

• • •

I waited in the reception of Xera Solutions for over an hour. Rohit told me they would make me wait to test my patience. But little did they know that they were dealing with someone who had had two tablespoons of patience before breakfast every day for the past four-and-a-half years.

I wore a light blue shirt and formal black pants that had a textured finish. I had worn a tie too, but Rohit told me I was overdoing it and forced me to remove it.

The office was on the top floor of a seven-storey building. There was a huge name board by the entrance, with the name Xera painted in dark orange and black on it.

The furniture, the walls and the other interiors had the orange-black theme as well. There was a large reception table that had a computer, a few landline phones and a pretty receptionist beside it, who multitasked between receiving phone calls, greeting people who walked in and entering data into the computer.

I glanced at her. She looked cute. She wore a pink shirt and formal white pants. Her pink lipstick matched the colour of her shirt, while her nail polish matched the colour of her pants. The most attractive thing was she wore was a smile that never ceased to appear whenever someone greeted her. The telephone before her rang. I watched her closely as she answered it and spoke to the person on the other end with that lovely smile. It all appeared to be in slow motion. She gently placed the receiver back and glanced at me. I knew she realised I was staring at her. But I didn't care.

"Are you Abhishek Krishnan?" she asked. I gulped. I stopped slow-motion-gazing.

How did she know me? She must have seen me in some college cultural event in Chennai. She must have been one of my fans, I convinced myself.

"Errr... yes," I said.

"Please go to cabin number three. Someone from the team will meet you there." she said.

She did not fail to smile. I realised I was overthinking.

"Sure. Thanks," I said and rose.

She also rose to open the door to the main office using her access card. She held the door open for me and gestured to me to go inside.

"The third room to your right," she directed me.

I inhaled the smell of her strong perfume as I walked past her. It was as though the perfume was made just for her.

"Thanks," I said. She smiled again.

"Good luck," she said.

"Thanks again." I smiled.

• • •

"Tell me something about yourself." The pretty lady in cabin number 3 asked me.

She was in her late twenties and looked extremely well-to-do. She had straightened hair that fell a little below her shoulders. She wore a sparkling white shirt along with a dark blue formal skirt. Her nails and eyebrows were as neatly-shaped as her perfect body.

"Well, I am Abhishek Krishnan from Chennai. I am a visual communications graduate. I like doing stuff that I am passionate about. I may appear like a man of a few words to the people I just meet. That's how I am initially. It takes me time to get close to people. Maybe I took my parents' advice not to talk to strangers too seriously as a kid."

She laughed.

"Why is that?" she asked, pushing the words through her laughter.

"I don't know. It just doesn't come to me naturally. I just can't think of what to say beyond a 'hello' and a 'how are you.' I admire people who strike conversations just like that," I said, snapping my fingers.

I liked the way she watched me talk. She glanced at my shoulders and hands as I shrugged and snapped during my over-animated chatter. From her expression, I got the feeling that she appeared interested in listening to me. So I decided to continue.

"Some people just come up to me and say *God, it's so hot outside* or *it's raining so hard*. I understand that they are trying to strike up a conversation with me. But, in my mind

I would be like, '*Yeah, I can see that too. So*' I kind of feel awkward when it comes to making conversations of that sort with new people.

My mind would want to discuss many things. But I get the feeling that people would judge me. For instance, when I see a girl with beautiful eyes, I really feel like going and telling her that. But I obviously won't. Because she might put me on the 'eve teasers' list. However, a clever person would first start a conversation with her and talk about her eyes only after she gets comfortable. That is my issue. I barely know how to start a conversation with a stranger. I tend to talk only when it is absolutely necessary. Otherwise, it's more of listening and observation."

She listened to me patiently.

"But do you realise you've been doing more talking than observing right here."

I laughed.

"Yes. But you started the conversation. And yeah, I was observing as I spoke."

She seemed surprised.

"*Ahan.* Can you tell me what you observed?"

"Ummm... you are wearing contact lenses. The right corner of your lower lip moves slightly to the side when you speak. And you look beautiful."

She laughed and blushed at the same time.

"Now, that's some observation. And thank you." The blush did not leave her face.

She glanced at my resume.

"Abhishek, I see that you have had four idle years after college. Why is that? Were you doing a course that you have missed mentioning?"

I took a moment to think of an answer.

"Was I doing a course? Yes. I did a non-certified course in Passionology. You learn about how passion can make you stupid and how people can take advantage of your ambition.

The duration of the course depends on the depth of your passion and stupidity."

Her eyes demanded an elaboration. I delivered a short synopsis of my flashback.

"Oh! So, I am talking to an upcoming superstar," she said.

"Maybe," I said.

"But Abhishek do you realise that by recruiting you, we would expect you to work with us at least for a year. What if you just leave us one fine day?"

"Well, I wouldn't do that." I lied. "You know how cinema is. You can't make it so easily. Moreover, I have decided to put all movie-related activities on hold for a good couple of years. That is why I am sitting here, in front of you today."

"Fair enough. Okay, Abhishek. I like your profile and the way you talk. Since you do not have experience in a BPO, I will have to take you in as a fresher. Your salary will be basic. Fifteen thousand rupees. Is that okay with you?"

Well, that's a start. I thought.

"Sure. Good for me," I said.

"Okay then. I'll see you soon. Thank you," she said and gave me a handshake.

"My pleasure. Ummm... what's your name again?"

"Sushmita Banerjee. I will be your process and accent trainer," she said.

"Banerjee. Are you Bengali?"

"Yes."

"Well, that explains your fish-shaped eyes."

"I'll take that as a compliment." She blushed.

"It was," I said, smiling.

"Okay. Meet you on the other side of Xera Solutions."

"Yup. I'll wait for the call. Bye."

• • •

"Dude, were you flirting with her?"

We were at a restaurant in BTM layout having dinner together.

"Of course not," I said, as soon as I swallowed the piece of paratha I had put in my mouth. "She is cute. I just told her what I felt about her."

"Did you tell her that her eyes were fish-shaped?"

"Yes. They are. Aren't they? And it was a compliment.

Was that wrong?" I asked.

"Not really. I guess she liked the compliment. She told me that she just realised that her eyes were fish-shaped."

"There you go." I put another piece of *paratha* in my mouth and glanced at my plate. "I think I like her," I said, without looking up.

"Whoa, whoa, whoa. Easy there, boy. She is a tough lady. You will know when your training starts," he said.

"I can't wait," I said.

"Cheque please," Rohit requested. "Dude. I've got to run back to the office. You get back to our room and get some sleep. I will meet you tomorrow morning," he said, dropping the room key on the table.

"Sure. Have fun," I said.

"Fun? It's been a tough month, brother. The sales count has been low. I am working on a root cause analysis document," he said.

"Whatever that means," I said, shrugging.

"I'll see you tomorrow."

"Yup."

I put on my jacket and walked out of the restaurant. It was pretty cold, and the road invited me for a walk. Although our PG was just behind the restaurant, I decided to take the longer route around it. There is nothing like a long and refreshing walk to clear thoughts about your past. A drop of rain fell on my face. I looked up. The night sky was dark and cloudy. I had many brighter clouds around me in the past. Shruthi, Peri, Chalu and all my friends back in college. The wind of life made them all pass.

Maybe that is how life is. Clouds, whether bright or dark, they just keep passing. The duration they stay with us depends on whether the circumstances around us are breezy, windy or stormy.

I reached our room. It was 9 PM. I wanted to call home and tell them the news they had been longing to hear. Just as I took my phone out, I received another call. It was from an unknown number.

"Hello," I answered the call.

"Hello. Is this Abhishek?"

"Yes."

"Hi, this is Vanita calling you from Srish Films. This is in reply to the pictures you sent us a month ago," she said.

"Okayyy," I said, eagerly expecting her to continue.

"Well, there is a Bollywood project that is to kick off in a couple of months. And the director is interested in casting you in the film. Would you be interested?"

My heart rate shot up like a rocket.

"Well, yes of course. Can you give me the details?" I said, my heart panting heavily.

"I have emailed you the details. Please take a look at it. I will call you back tomorrow. I am sorry to have called you at unofficial hours. We are in a bit of a hurry."

"That's absolutely fine. I will check my email and wait for your call." I said.

Bollywood. Wow. I told myself.

I quickly grabbed Rohit's laptop from his table and opened my email. There was a mail from the email address '8000vanitha@gmail.com'.

KINDLY FIND THE ATTACHMENT

NOTE: IT IS DIRECT CASTING, NO AUDITION, KINDLY NOTE WE ARE BANNER WE ARE NOT AGENTS.

IF YOU HAVE MAIL YOUR PHOTOS AND BIO DATA, FOR SELECTION STATUS KINDLY CONTACT

CASTING DIRECTOR

VANITA K.S.FILMS Presentation SRISH FILMS PRODUCTION

Banner registered with WESTERN INDIA FILM PRODUCER ASSOCIATION, Vide ID no.: 11345

Office L/801, RNA Regency Park, Kandivali West, Mumbai - 400067, Maharashtra State, India

We Are Into The Business Of High-Quality Commercial Feature Film.

I read the mail thoroughly, overlooking the grammar errors. I opened the attachment. It was a PDF file that had the following details in it:

Welcome everyone. Allow us to present to you all, our most ambitious Hindi film project

A thrilling Hindi horror feature film to be shot with the latest 3D stereography technology.

A P. ANIL KUMAR Presentation A Srish Films production

A Horror Thriller that will take you to the edge of your seat

A story about 12 best friends who fight 4 living dead creatures to save their friendship!

A challenge of the demons who want to hunt for blood...

Friendship will be put to the test in that grilling one night that goes wrong

Will the friendship stand the test of time when everyone's life is in danger?

To be filmed in the deadliest locations abroad

With 16 actors who will touch the heights of performance

Witness the breathtaking story

No one fears the dead, until they rise back.

6 Friends... 4 Dead Bodies... 1 Abandoned Bungalow.

THE LOST SHADOW

A thrilling Hindi horror feature film Written and Directed by Aji Sandhu

Produced by P. Sakshi Tulasi & Shreya Sandhu Music by Sammy Joshua & Hitesh Gadasia Executive Producer: Malaika Danish

Action: Hinder Singh Cinematography: Pranesh Patel Casting Director: Vanita

Post-Production: Race Media

Coming soon to create chills in theatres worldwide

The document also contained a synopsis of the movie and a brief profile of the director. It looked pretty presentable, and I felt bells ringing inside me. I did not have the patience to wait until the next day. I called Vanita back immediately.

"This seems interesting. How do we take this forward?" I asked her.

"Okay, first of all Abhishek, you would be playing an important role and your remuneration would be 10 lacs."

My eyes widened when she said that.

"Do you have a passport?" she asked.

"Yes. I do." I said.

"Great. We will be shooting in New Zealand for two months. You will have to come to Mumbai in a week to sign the agreement. Please text me your address I will courier you the flight tickets."

My head started spinning already. This was definitely my ticket to fame. Just as I thought the doors were closing, I had been directed to a bigger door.

"Okay. I'll do that," I said.

"Perfect. So this is going to be simple. You will have to pay us a security deposit of fifty thousand rupees because we are investing so much on you. Your tickets and visa and all. This amount is hundred percent refundable. You can count on us," she said.

My head spun fast. Paying fifty thousand was not only way too far from possible, but also against the 'no-more-paying-for-acting' policy I had initiated. I realised I had to end the conversation right there.

"Not happening, Vanita. I can't afford that amount. I guess I'll bail out. Thanks for calling," I said, trying to be straightforward.

"I understand. But do think it over. We are hundred percent genuine. We have provided all our details in the email itself. If anything wrong happens, you can come straight down to our office."

"No Vanita. I don't want to do this," I said.

"Okay then. There are a couple of Telugu projects that I am working on. I will let you know if there are opportunities for you in them," she said and hung up.

I couldn't sleep that night. Not only because it was raining and the cold had seeped in but also because the phone call had pushed away the thick blanket I had used to cover my passion, waking it up in the process.

I had various thought bubbles swirling around my head.

Fifty thousand rupees. There was no way I was going to get so much money. Okay, wait. If God really wants me to take this up, he would have constructed a route to get to the money too. Let me just give this a try. If I get the money, it means God wants me to take this. If not, I'll just let it go.

The thoughts just kept reappearing. I finally decided to give it a shot.

• • •

"Rohit, I need help," I said, as soon as he stepped into our room and refreshed himself.

"What?"

"Is there any possibility for you to lend me fifty thousand rupees?"

I had been sleeplessly thinking of where to start from and I decided to ask Rohit first. However, I made it a point that I wouldn't tell him the actual reason until it happened.

"50K!" he exclaimed, his eyes growing round.

"Yes. There is an emergency at home. My dad called last night," I lied.

He thought for a while.

"I have invested all my money in savings. Wait, let me think. Ummm... maybe I can get a salary advance. But fifty thousand is not really possible. I might be able to get around thirty."

Thirty is fine, I thought. *I could either convince Vanita or borrow another twenty thousand from someone else.*

"Thirty should be good. Something is better than nothing, right?" I said.

"Cool. Thirty it is then. I'll talk about it to the office and let you know by tomorrow," he said.

"Sounds good. I will repay this in a couple of months.

Thank you so much, buddy."

"Shut up and let me sleep now," he said, with a smile.

I smiled too. I had one more task to accomplish. Call Vanita and convince her. I checked the time. It was 4:00 AM. If I called her that early in the morning, she would have buried me in the pine forests of New Zealand. I decided to get some sleep.

• • •

"Thirty thousand shouldn't be a problem," Vanita said. "It is a refundable amount anyway. We just need some kind of a surety. That's it."

I was speaking to her from the balcony, after making sure Rohit was not able to hear my conversation.

"Perfect," I said.

"I will send you the account details. Please deposit the money in a couple of days. I will let you know when we courier the flight tickets," she said.

I already felt myself on a plane en route Mumbai, en route cinema, en route fame. I couldn't believe all this was happening. I felt on top of the world.

• • •

I transferred the cash in a couple of days. I still hadn't received a call from Xera Solutions confirming my joining date. But in another couple of days, Vanita called.

"Abhishek, do you have a card at the actors' union?" she asked.

"No. I don't have one," I said, standing on the balcony of our PG, glancing into the room every now and then to make sure Rohit was still asleep.

"Oops. I was under the assumption that you had one. I am sorry, Abhishek. We will refund the money. We will not be able to cast you," she said.

The plane that I was travelling on began to lose altitude. I did not want a life jacket. I wanted to take the plane all the way to its destination.

"Is there a way out?" I asked.

"Yes. We can help you get a card. But that will cost you ten thousand rupees."

Now, I had a situation. The demand for extra money somehow began to make me feel suspicious. I didn't know if I was being trapped again?

Okay, I'll ask her for a couple of days' time. I will not even try for the money. But if it still comes to me, I will take it as a green signal. If not, I will just ask for a refund. I decided in my mind.

"Abhishek, are you there?" Vanita asked, reacting to my long pause.

"Can I tell you in two days, Vanita?" I asked.

"Okay," she said, after thinking for a moment. "But please transfer the money in two days, or else we will have to move on. We are running late already."

She appeared a little sharp-tongued for the first time.

"Sure," I said.

Okay, listen. I told myself. *This is all programmed. I am yet to receive a call from Xera. I am almost in a Hindi film. This means God wants me to go after my passion. I'll wait for a couple of days. The money will come to me like a miracle.*

• • •

Three days had passed. I neither got a call from Xera nor did that expected miracle happen. Rohit told me that they were interviewing a few other candidates before they could put us all into a training batch. I did not worry about it much because I was more excited about the horror movie I was going to do.

But, to my horror, Vanita called and informed me that they wouldn't be able to wait any longer.

"I trusted you, Abhishek," she said as though I was in a relationship with her and was two-timing her. "I kept the producer waiting, expecting you to revert in a couple of days. Now, I have clearly been informed that you will neither be in the project nor will you get the refund."

She was extremely rude. She hung up midway. I tried calling her back. She did not answer. I tried all day. Her phone was soon switched off. I did not want a role in the movie. I just wanted my money back. I called her the entire day. Her phone never came back on.

I realised that this was another money snatching tactic mastered by a bunch of fraudsters. I did not have the strength to go after them. My passion made me blind again. I was deeply disappointed. More so, because I had lied to Rohit to get the money. I had to repay him at the earliest to shed the guilt. Just as I wondered what I was going to do, I got a call from Xera Solutions. They gave me my joining date, pulling me away from my dreams and shoving me into reality. I had three days time to put away all the disappointment and begin a new life. It was too short a time. But I had no choice.

• • •

I opened the door into the work area of Xera Solutions using the access card I was given along with my appointment letter. I did not fail to greet the receptionist at the entrance and earn an adorable smile from her. I wore a white shirt and navy blue pants. I recollected my revulsion towards corporate life and formal attire that I talked to Jesse about a few years ago. I had always said that my life would start and end on a movie set.

Unfortunately, at the moment, I had to consider the corporate office as my movie set, where I had to act without pre-written script lines. I had to pretend I was happy there. I had to act as though I loved sales. I had to act before my customers as though I was working hard for their satisfaction.

Well, the training started. I was introduced to a few other boys and girls in my training batch, who were mostly younger than me. I soon learned that we were going to work for a UK client, who dealt with mobile networks. We were to pitch new mobile packages to T-Mobile, Vodafone and 3 Network customers according to their usage. But before we were trained in the process, we had to undergo accent training. Sushmita, our trainer, was absolute eye candy.

"Hello... How azh y' all?" she asked, throwing in an accent.

Her face looked fresh, as though she had just taken it out of a refrigerator. She had absolutely no make-up on and still looked dazzling.

"Fine. Thank you," I said while the others glanced at each other wondering whether to answer her or just nod their heads.

"How was yozh weeken'd?"

"It was great. How was yours?" I said while a few whispered a 'good' and the others just stuck to nodding their heads.

"Do I look like a ghost? Why are you all acting funny?" she asked, ignoring me and my question.

No. You look like an angel dressed in formal clothes. I wanted to tell her. I wanted to do a lot of things. But I resolved to focus on training.

"We've got to do some talking if this training has to stay alive," she said, with a sweet smile.

Everyone grinned widely, as I smacked my lips at her deliciousness. I was attracted to her. I wanted to see more of her to stay alive.

"So let's begin with your names," she said.

• • •

The training started off in full swing. Sushmita gave us tips on how to change our accent a bit to sound convincingly neutral.

"You've gotta roll yozh R's, kiss yozh W's aan'd bite yozh V's," she said. "Say aaazhh."

"Aaarrrr," we shouted in unison.

"Aaaazzhh," she corrected us. "You've gotta zholl yozh tongue inwards."

"Aaaaarrrzzzzhhh." We croaked, rolling our tongues in like mattresses, touching our tonsils in the process.

"Okay, that will need some pzhactice," she said, with a serious face. "Now say oowhat."

"Vaat?" It was more of a question than a recital from us.

"Oowhat. You've gotta puckezh yozh lips for W like you'zh kissing someone. Kiss yozh Ws."

She spoke with an accent during the entire training session and we had quite a tough time following her instructions. After a good four hours of tongue exercise, she checked her watch.

"Okay. Let's break for dinner," she said.

Everyone sprung out of their seats and threw themselves out of the training room, dragging their tongues along with them. Sushmita sat on her chair. I saw her, still sitting on my chair. I waited for her to look at me and as soon as she did, I began to look around as though searching for something.

"Lost something?" she asked.

"Well, yes. I was just searching for the Sushmita I met at the interview," I said.

She smiled.

"Why? Don't I have fish-shaped eyes anymore?" she quipped.

"You do. But you're so strict."

"That's how I am in training mode," she said.

"It's surprising how you manage to switch modes so easily," I said.

"You'll start adapting, you'll see," she said.

She looked a little tired after the four-hour long session.

"You don't want to have dinner?" I asked.

"I am not hungry. I think I'll get myself some coffee." She stood up and walked towards the door. She stopped by the exit and turned around.

"You want to join?" she asked, her voice sounding formal.

"I thought you would never ask," I said.

I stood up and followed her towards the cafeteria.

• • •

Sushmita and I grabbed our cups of coffee from the counter. Xera Solutions had a huge cafeteria that had a seating capacity of at least fifty. The tables were round and were of different colours. There were different food counters that suited everyone's taste, appetite and mood. The smells of the different varieties of food met at a commonplace, before blending with each other and hitting the nostrils of the visitors.

People used Sodexo coupons that were issued by the company, to get themselves whatever they wanted to munch on. Sushmita used her coupons for both our cups of coffee. There was an open place beside the cafeteria, which was used as a smoking zone.

Xera Solutions was on the seventh floor of the building, and the smoking zone was bliss. There was a breeze blowing in all the time, so much that people had to resort to Zippo lighters to light their cigarettes. It was an amazing feeling to experience the sight of the city from a silent distance. There were ashtrays and coffee mug holders placed beside benches positioned at appropriate distances from one another.

Sushmita walked straight into the smoking zone and found an isolated corner. I followed her like an obedient student.

"Smoke?" she asked, offering me a cigarette.

"No. I don't smoke," I said, rejecting her offer.

She placed the cigarette between her lips and lit it using a lighter.

"Do you drink?" she asked, as she took a puff.

"Nope. I am a teetotaler," I said.

"That's nice."

I knew she was trying to keep a conversation going, but I was preoccupied with observing her intriguing mannerisms. She alternated between sipping coffee and taking a puff. I noticed that she placed her cigarette only at the corner of her lips.

"I like your style," I said, after thinking for a while if it was okay to say it.

"The other day it was my eyes and lips. Now it is my style. Huh? What's all this about?"

Although she tried to make it sound adorable, I could sense she was trying to hold a line between us, which I thought was appropriate, because we had just met.

"This is scratch-back policy," I said, taking a moment to come up with the term.

She checked her watch.

"I guess I've got time to understand what scratch-back policy is," she said, her fish-shaped eyes demanding an explanation.

"Well, a scratch-back policy is a practice where I tell you something good about you so that I can hear something good about me in return. Haven't you heard of the phrase, I scratch your back and you scratch mine?"

She lifted her eyebrows as she took a sip of coffee.

"So, you want me to say something nice about you?"

I nodded my head.

"Why?"

"Because I am an actor. I always look for appreciation. I am like a dog craving attention."

"You are such a girl," she said, as she dropped her cigarette butt.

"Hey guys." A voice came from behind us.

It was Rohit. He walked up to us with a glass of fresh orange juice and a cigarette.

"I was looking for you inside. What's happening?" he asked.

"I was just learning a few new terms from your friend," Sushmita said.

"*Ahan*. What's that?" Rohit asked.

Sushmita narrated my scratch-back policy story.

"He has scratched my back quite a few times. And apparently, it's my turn now."

Rohit looked at me as though he would stick his cigarette up my nose any moment. I turned around, so my back was to Sushmita.

"Just a small scratch would do for the moment," I said. She burst out laughing.

"I can't think of anything now. I'll tell you when training ends," she said.

"Fair enough," I said.

"Okay. I am hungry now. Let's get something to eat," Sushmita said.

As she stepped forward, her high heels swayed to one side, making her lose balance. She began to fall. I quickly stepped forward and held her as she gently fell on my arms. She was as light as a feather. Her body felt incredibly soft. Her hair brushed against my thighs. I had one hand behind her back and the other one holding her hip.

I looked into her face. It felt like I was carrying a bundle of cotton that had a cute baby face. I glanced at her eyes. They were tired and reddish. I so wanted to hold her closer to me and put her to sleep. But I wanted to kiss her first. I don't know why I was so attracted to her. I was quite sure I wasn't in love with her. But I wanted to be around her.

"Thank you. You just saved my life," she teased.

She held my arms tightly and gathered some support to stand up, digging her fingernails into my elbow in the process.

I wish you lost balance all the time. I wanted to tell her this.

Just as that thought ran through my mind, she slipped again. My arms automatically followed her hip and back, but she managed to balance herself to their disappointment. She walked into the cafeteria and I followed her, hoping she would fall again.

• • •

Sushmita got back to trainer mode as soon as she stepped into the training room. The button that was supposed to transform me into student mode did not work. I was in no mood of rolling my Rs or kissing my Ws. I wanted to gaze at her although my sleepy eyes began to betray me. I wished she was my W. She would have instructed me to kiss her then. I was so lost in thought that I did not realise my drowsy brain had pushed me off my seat making me fall on the floor with a thud.

The impact of the thud did not wake me up. I was so sleepy that my eyes simply refused to open and look at Sushmita. It was darkness all over again. My brain offered to show her to me in my dreams. I liked the deal. Just as I clicked the "okay" button, I felt water being sprinkled on my face. My eyes were forced open to find Sushmita kneeling in front of me, staring at me with frightened eyes. Her hair tickled my face. I quickly sat up and glanced at her as though I was struck with amnesia.

"Thank you. You just saved my life," I said, smiling.

She slapped my elbow.

"You scared me," she said.

"I... I just fell asleep. Not used to night shift," I said.

The other trainees laughed. Sushmita participated in the laughter too.

"You've got to get used to it kiddo" she said, brushing my hair.

"May be from tomorrow. Let me sleep now pleeeaaase." I made a cute puppy face.

"I told you. You are such a girl. You can use the dormitory," she said.

"The girl's dormitory?" I asked, putting on an excited face.

"You wish," she said. "Let's stop training for today. You guys can rest. We'll start fresh tomorrow."

"Oowow. That's gzheat," we cheered in unison. Sushmita laughed.

"But remember. We can't afford to do this from tomorrow," she said.

"Suzhe ma'am," I said.

15

Back to Chennai

I woke up to the sound of the SMS on my mobile. I was so used to the sound now that it could wake me up from sleep at any hour of the night or day.

It was an SMS from Shruthi.

Abi. There is a problem. Dad has doubts about our relationship. He has taken my mobile. I just snuck into his room to send you this message. See you at the beach at 4 p.m. as planned. Remember, I will not have my mobile. Be there on time. I will wait by the Gandhi statue. More details when we meet. Luv you. Bye. Don't reply.

I saw this coming right from the time her dad gave me a doubtful look on her birthday. But I did not expect it to happen this fast. Maybe it was time to tell her dad about us or maybe not.

It was five in the morning, which meant I had a good eleven hours to decide whether to tell her dad or not. I put the phone back under my pillow and covered my head with the blanket.

In what seemed like a few minutes, my phone buzzed again. It wasn't an SMS this time. It was a call. My hands did what it would do, by default.

"Yes, Shruthi," I answered the call.

I heard a male voice from the other end. It took a moment for me to realise that it wasn't her.

"Who is this?" I said.

"It's me. Rohit."

I frowned. Not because I did not know who Rohit was but because I really did not expect a call from him at half-past-five in the morning.

"Dude!!! How are you?" I was obviously surprised by his call.

"Bad news, bro. My dad passed away early this morning. He had a stroke."

"What???" I was shell-shocked.

"Yes. The cremation is in the evening. Come if possible. Same place. Saligramam."

I couldn't utter a word. He hung up before I could respond.

Rohit was my school mate and a super close friend. We had spent a lot of time at each other's house during school. We were in the same batch and played together in the school cricket team. His father was extremely fond of me. I spent most of my 12th grade board exam study holidays at his house. His dad even gifted me a watch, a day before the board exams.

"Keep running, Abi. Time will wait for none." Those were the last words he said to me as far as I could remember. The memories made multitudinous orbits around my head. It was strange how our brains picked up random events when we tried to recollect something. Rohit and I promised to keep in touch even after school. But the new clouds that engulfed us kept us apart. I didn't even remember where I had put the watch his dad had gifted me.

• • •

I looked at my watch as I walked to the bike parking area, after having been with Rohit through the funeral. It was six in the evening and I suddenly remembered that I had promised to meet Shruthi at 4 p.m. I whacked my own head. I sucked at keeping promises. I took my mobile phone out. I noticed about 45 missed calls from an unknown landline number. I had kept my mobile phone on silent as I thought it was appropriate to do so in the bereaved aura. I called her mobile.

"Hello." It was a male voice.

I winced, realising too late that her phone was with her dad.

"Shruthi. Your friend's short film has been edited. I am not able to get in touch with him. Please ask him to get in touch with me," I said, trying to sound formal and academic.

"This is her dad. I am out now. I will let Shruthi know once I get home." He hung up abruptly.

I blew out a mouth full of steaming carbon dioxide. I stared at an image of Shruthi, who stared back at me from my mobile phone.

All the ice that had kept my head cool for so long metamorphosed into liquid form and showed up in my eyes.

"I am sorry, baby," I said.

She looked at me and smiled. I knew she was burning on the inside.

• • •

I made my way through the peak-hour traffic of Chennai. I wanted to get to her house in Anna Nagar before her father got there. I wanted to look into her eyes and tell her I was sorry.

What if her dad got there before I did? What if he lied that he was outside?

These questions chased and caught up with me as I raced my Activa to the maximum capacity the Honda engineers had designed it for. I did not care if her father was there. I would open up to him about our relationship and ask his daughter's hand. I was determined.

I practised dialogues to deliver to her dad during the rest of my journey.

• • •

I jogged through the compound of her two-storey house and hit the door bell. The determination that I pulled up on my way abandoned me at the gate to her house. I did not want her dad to be around or her grandmother. I rang her doorbell a couple more times. The atmosphere was dark and silent except for the lights by the gate.

I could hear footsteps approaching the door. I listened closely. I could hear the sound of her thin anklets. I shut my eyes and anticipated the smell of her fragrance when she opened the door. A gust of perfume hit my face. I opened my eyes and looked at her.

She was wearing a white *kameez* along with white *patiala* pants. She had matched all her accessories with the colour of her clothes — white bindi, white bangles, white earrings and a white beaded chain. She was wearing more *kajal* than usual. She was the perfect definition of the word 'angel'.

Her lips quivered the moment she saw me. She turned around and walked in, leaving the door open.

Was she calling me in?

I answered my own question in the affirmative. I stepped in all tired and famished after a long day.

"Shruthi."

"Go away," she said. Her voice sounded weak.

"Shruthi, my friend's dad passed away. I had to..."

"You could have told me," she interrupted.

Her voice got weaker.

"You asked me not to call you." I tried defending myself.

"I called you a million times."

My defence was in vain. I had no answer. Her eyes welled up. The last thing I wanted was to see her cry.

"Listen baby. I have been having a very bad day. I get your SMS about your dad. My friend's dad passes away. I see my friend and his family in tears. I keep you waiting for me for hours. I almost get you in trouble by calling your dad. Now I see you cry. I can't take this any more, baby."

She did not reply. She stood facing the wall, showing me her back.

"Go," she said.

May be I should leave her alone and talk to her later, I thought.

"Fine. I am leaving," I said, softly and walked away hesitantly.

She quickly held my hand that was placed on the wall beside the door. She rested her wet cheek on the back of my palm. I glanced at her. She looked adorable even when she was crying.

"You have no clue for how long I waited. People began to stare at me suspiciously. It felt really awful."

"I am sorry, baby. I understand what you would have gone through." I couldn't tell her anything else.

There was a moment of silence.

"I understand what you would have gone through too," she said and buried her face in my chest.

All the *kajal* from her eyes smudged onto my white shirt. I caressed her hair and kissed her forehead. I wiped her tears and held her chin.

"I have a weak heart. I really can't see you in tears although you look beautiful when you cry," I said.

"I love you," she said and hugged me.

"I love you too."

"And by the way, it was me who you spoke to over the phone. Not my dad. He gave my phone back to me before he left."

I was surprised.

"But the voice?"

"You mean *this voice?*" She spoke in a convincing male voice.

"You are one hell of a prankster. Aren't you?" I said and poked her stomach softly.

She jumped back and shrieked. She pulled my cheeks and gave me a little peck.

"I thought kitchen closes only by midnight," I teased.

"Go away," she said, pretending to be strict.

I pulled her closer to me and kissed her lips. She hugged me tightly as we kissed.

"Okay. Let me get out of here before Hulk Hogan returns," I said.

"Bye. Call me once you get home."

"Sure." I gave her another tiny peck on her lips and left.

• • •

16

Pridification

It took me about fifteen days to get used to the night shift. Our accent training was over and we stepped into process training. Sushmita gave us call scripts and asked us to memorise them.

"This is your Bible, guys. Read through it. You will be delivering exactly these lines when you speak to a customer," she said as she walked up and down the training room, passing in front of my chair every now and then.

I inhaled her scent deep into my lungs each time she walked past me. I began to like everything about her — her attitude, her personality, her looks, her voice. It had just been over a fortnight and I had already started developing strong feelings for her. I made sure I went out for breaks and stuck around her all the time. We even took long walks in the lonely streets after work. I liked to make her laugh and she seemed to like my company.

The next fifteen days of training were hardcore, but it was fun because she was around. I continued to shower her with my rib ticklers and I enjoyed watching her laugh to glory. I once narrated our light music onstage experience during our college days and she sat on the road for over a minute, holding her stomach laughing. In the one month I was with her, she had fully learned about my past, while I started having ideas of making a future with her. I did not ask her anything about her life or her past. All I knew was that her parents were in Kolkata, she lived alone in Bangalore and that she was single.

"Dude, do you know where Sushmita is?" I asked Rohit as I walked past his cubicle.

It was dinner time on our last day of training. Sushmita left our training room an hour before break time, telling us she would be right back. However, she did not turn up.

"Nope. Is everything alright?" he asked.

"I think so," I said and explained her sudden disappearance.

"She must be on a call or something dude. Go check in the cafeteria," he said.

"Okay. When are you coming for dinner?" I asked.

"I've got a client call in a minute. I should be there in fifteen minutes," he said.

"Alright. See you there."

I walked straight through the cafeteria into the smoking zone. I skimmed my eyes through the regular visitors and found Sushmita standing in a dark corner. She wasn't smoking. She was staring at the city. I walked up to her.

"Are you okay?" I asked.

She was startled by my voice. She turned around to face me. She had tears in her eyes. I was alarmed. I did not expect her to be teary-eyed. I did not know how to react.

"Oh no. Y-you are crying. D-do you want me to leave you alone?" I said and started to walk away.

"No, it's okay," she said. "Is there anything important?"

"Not really. I just thought we'd have dinner together."

"I'll be right there in a minute."

I looked at her closely. She had been crying so much that her tears had wet her lovely pink shirt. She took out a cigarette and her lighter. She tried to light it but the breeze just did not let her do that. She attempted it a few times and threw the lighter away in anger. I took the lighter from the floor and took a step closer to her, preventing the breeze from blowing the flame out.

"See, when there is resistance, nothing can let you down," I said as I helped her light her cigarette.

She smiled.

"Thank you," she said.

"Now tell me. Are you angry or upset?"

There was a moment of silence. I was not sure if I was making her uncomfortable. I could see that her eyes were brimming up again. She wiped them away.

"Both," she said and took a long drag from her cigarette. I waited for her to exhale all the smoke.

"I was married."

I looked at her as though she had just said that I had gotten her pregnant. She observed my reaction.

"Yes, Abhishek. I was married to an asshole. He just did not like me talking to guys. Initially, I thought he was being possessive. But I soon learned that he doubted me for everything I did. There were days when he locked me inside the house, stopping me from getting to the office. I even hated having sex with him. He treated me like a fucking prostitute. I applied for divorce in a couple of months. It's been a year since we have been separated and this bastard just called me to ask how many people I slept with in this one year."

I glanced at her struck with a praralysed tongue. I couldn't believe she had such a terrible past. Why are such psychopaths even alive?

"I haven't really unveiled my past to anybody here. But I feel comfortable around you. This is between us, okay?"

"Goes without saying. You are a brave girl, Sushmita. I admire your strength," I said, not knowing what else to say to console her.

"Is this part of your scratch-back policy?" she asked, with a tiny trace of a smile at the corner of her lips.

I wanted to capitalise on that smile.

"No, this is *pridification*."

She laughed.

"Pridi-whaat?"

"Pridification. It is a process where you remind a person about the great things she does whenever she is down. Remind her of how courageous she has been to fight the odds and come a long way. Make her proud of herself. It's just been a month since we know each other. But I am really proud of you, Sushmita."

Our eyes met. By the look in her eyes, I felt that she wanted to kiss me. At least that is what I wanted to believe. I would have kissed her if there was nobody around.

"Looks like your shirt has been crying with you too," I said, pointing at the wet area around her shoulders.

She laughed. I couldn't control myself watching her adorable behaviour. I was addicted to her laughter.

"I am beginning to like you," I said.

She stopped laughing almost immediately. She obviously didn't see that coming. She stared at me as though I was asking her for her lungs. But all I wanted was her heart.

"What do you mean?"

"What I said. I am beginning to like you," I repeated.

I had really wanted to tell her this and I was glad I did. I did not even care that I could lose my job because of this. Sushmita continued to look at me without blinking.

"I-I'm sorry. I am kind of not getting you here. Are you asking me out?"

My heart performed Bharatanatyam inside my rib cage.

"Yes Sushmita, I am beginning to have strong feelings for you. It really feels good to be with you all the time. I am so addicted to your laughter that I just want to keep seeing you laugh."

She blushed, yet there was an unsettled look in her eyes. She was probably wondering how to respond. She took a while to examine my face.

"You are a nice chap, Abi," she said, finally.

I noticed that she had called me 'Abi' for the first time. Generally only the people close to me called me that. I blushed too.

"I really do like being with you too. But, you know, I am not too keen about any kind of a commitment. I don't even want to marry again."

"I completely understand that, Sush," I said, taking the liberty to be less formal.

We looked at each other for a moment. There was an awkward silence.

"Well, let's just do what our hearts want us to and see how it goes," she said, breaking the silence.

I shrugged, nodded and smiled at her. She dropped her cigarette and blew out the final batch of smoke from her chimney.

"Looks like you've finally blown out all that steam you had earlier," I joked.

She laughed again.

"Why does your cigarette smell different from the others?" I asked, sniffing a bit of the smoke before it escaped into the city.

"Because this is not tobacco. It's weed," she said hesitantly.

"What the fuck! All these days you were smoking weed?" I asked, dumbfounded by her reply.

"Yes, kiddo." She brushed my hair again. I really did feel like a kid.

"That explains your red eyes and slippery feet!" I exclaimed, as though I had just caught a monkey stealing cookies.

"Yes, baby. This has been a great help in my pridification process," she said with a smirk.

"That reminds me of something you promised," I said. I gave a moment for her to recollect her promise.

"What did I promise?" She didn't even try to think.

"Today is the last day of training. You promised to scratch my back today," I said.

"Yesss. I remember. But training is not over yet. We still have four hours to go. *Chalo*, let's get some dinner and start calling."

"Are you not going to fall?" I asked, stretching out my arms for her as she stepped forward.

"No I am not and you'd better not sleep." She slapped my elbow.

We had dinner along with Rohit and walked onto the call floor for the final session of training.

17

No Longer Hungry

Chalu and I walked into Landmark in Spencer Plaza, to buy a card for Poornima. After all the hard work, Poornima had finally started talking to Chalu.

He wanted to give her a card and a little gift for her birthday as an application to convert their friendship into love. He made numerous circles around the birthday cards rack trying to find a card that would solve two purposes: wish her happy birthday and indirectly convey that she meant a lot to him.

"Hurry up, *da*. I am starving," I said. "If you had made these circles around the idols in temples, the gods would have fulfilled your wish."

"Shut up. I am trying to concentrate," he said.

"Screw you. I am going to the food court. Come there once you are done."

• • •

As I ran my eyes down the menu, confused about what to choose, a chicken burger or a chicken puff, I got a call from Shruthi.

"Where are you?" she asked.

"Spencers. Food court," I said.

"Okay. I am coming there in 15 minutes. I need to talk to you." She seemed to be in a hurry.

I hung up and glanced back at the menu, trying to guess at the back of my mind why she wanted to meet me in a hurry.

"One veg sandwich please," I said, giving up on the choices of chicken.

I turned around and noticed Chalu coming down the escalator.

"Please make that two," I said.

As Chalu displayed the goodies he got his future girlfriend, I had a range of inevitable thoughts running in my head.

What was she going to tell me? Let's break up?

I don't love you anymore? I miss you?

Let's get married?

Let's elope?

The word 'elope' echoed through my head a number of times as I noticed Shruthi walking into the food court, dressed in a plain white t-shirt and blue jeans, with a travel bag in her hand. The echo turned into an earthquake when I learned that she was not alone. She was with a guy.

He looked like one of those rich, arrogant pampered guys who got whatever they pointed at. By his wobbling skin, it was quite evident that his fingers had pointed at sweet stalls and junk bunks as a kid.

He wore thick wayfarer glasses and an orange shirt, which he would have probably used his finger to get too.

"Abi, this is Vineeth. My dad's business partner's son," Shruthi said.

Ohkay. So what? I said in my mind. "Hello Vineeth. Nice to meet you."

He just shook my hand without saying a word. Maybe as a kid, he never pointed his fingers at school, where they taught basic manners.

"Vineeth and I are heading to Idukki. There's a dispute in the business. My dad's selling his estate to Vineeth's dad. We've got some papers to sign."

"How are you going?" I asked.

"Vineeth's car," she said.

I looked at him. He played with the keys to his expensive car with an 'I-am-rich' attitude on his face.

"Okay. But why did you come here?" I asked.

"Because I wanted to give you a hug before I left," she said in a tone that urged me to smother her.

She stretched out her arms inviting me to wrap myself around her. I wasn't too sure if it was sensible to hug her in public. But before my mind came up with a possible decision, I found my body wrapped tightly around hers.

"I love you," I said.

"I crave for you," she said.

"I'll miss you," I said.

"I don't want to go." Her adorable tone came back and I pulled her soft cheeks.

"Shruthi, we'll have to start now," Vineeth said.

I wanted to stuff his car keys in his mouth and shove his face into the popcorn maker.

"Okay, sweetheart. I'll see you in a couple of days," she said.

I kissed her hand. She placed her kissed hand on her lips.

"Drive safe," I said.

It was more like a warning to the pampered bean bag. She turned around to leave. Her hair hit my face. I wanted to grab her from behind and kiss the back of her neck.

Vineeth looked me in the eye and rotated his car key again. I did not care to look at him. I had my eyes fixed on Shruthi. I liked the way her hips swayed when she walked.

"Come back quick," I shouted after her.

She dropped her bag, turned around, ran towards me and threw herself on me. Her stomach touched mine as her breathing got heavy.

"That was very quick," I said.

"Shut up and hug me," she said.

I put my arm around her back and tightened my hold on her while pulling her closer to me.

"If only my dad didn't have a business partner, things would have been different," she said.

"Do you want to tell me something?" I asked as curiosity hit me when she spoke with less relevance to the current situation.

"Lots. That is why I came here. I didn't expect that fatso to walk in with me. I just hate him," she whispered into my ear.

"We'll talk when you come back, baby. Whatever it is, be a brave girl."

"I am. Just stick by my side always."

"I am stuck all over you," I said.

"Okay. Bye."

She pecked my cheek with her neatly-shaped red lips.

"Bye," I said.

When she walked away, my heart felt like a sponge immersed in water. I had never felt so heavy. I knew that she was going through an uncomfortable phase. I wanted to embrace her, hold her close to me and say "everything is going to be okay." I was sure that is exactly what she wanted that moment. I just couldn't wait for her to return.

I glanced at Chalu. He pointed at the sandwich. I was no longer hungry.

I just couldn't wait for her to return. I promised myself that I would never ever let go of her.

18

Sushmita

Our final four hours of training was the most interesting part. We had to go live on the call floor and speak to real customers. We had practised our script a million times on the numerous mock calls we did during our training.

There are two network options in the UK. Contract and Pay As You Go, just like postpaid and prepaid in India. Customers who have contract plans are offered a phone along with their contract. We were to call customers who were on contract and pitch them better plans. I wore my headphones and began to dial.

"Hello, this is James calling from phone talk on behalf of 3 network. How are you doing today?" I said, as soon as my first customer answered my call.

"Not interested," the customer said rudely and slammed his phone down cutting me off.

Whoa. That's a great start, I thought.

I dialled about fifty numbers after that and most of them did not even let me go past the 'how are you doing today' part of my script. Some people told me that they were on the Telephone Preference Service list and that I was not supposed to be calling them. After a couple of hours and at least sixty rejections, I finally managed to get to the second paragraph of my script.

"Mr. Roland, according to your current contract plan, you have 200 voice minutes and 400 text messages free of cost every month. Am I right Mr. Roland?" I asked.

"Yes. That's correct."

"Well, the plan I am offering you would give you 250 voice minutes and 500 text messages along with a brand new Samsung J700 Stylish Slider phone absolutely free of cost. How do you like this, Mr. Roland?"

"It sounds interesting. But I think I should stick to my current plan." he said.

"Mr. Roland, you won't believe this. There is a pop up on my screen at the moment that says that you have just won 30 video call minutes extra along with this plan. I am sure you wouldn't want to miss this," I said, with fake excitement in my tone.

The 30 video call minutes was there in the plan already. But I held it back to throw it at him separately just to make him feel special. And the plan seemed to work.

"Wow, okay. I'll take it," he said.

I now had to get his card details and confirm the purchase. I wasn't too sure if I could do it. I looked at Sushmita, who stood a few meters away from me monitoring us. She looked at me. I gave her a thumbs up. She ran up to me, excitedly. I put the call on mute.

"He is interested. Can you finish this purchase? I am nervous," I whispered to her.

She nodded her head. I un-muted the call.

"Perfect. Congratulations. I am happy for you. Can you hold on a moment while I transfer the call to the purchase department to get your phone shipped to you?"

"Alright."

I quickly passed the headphone to Sushmita, who skillfully collected all information from him, using her several years of experience. She hung up, punched the table in triumph and stood up.

"Wooohooo. Guys. Listen up," she shouted.

The people who were not calling turned around to listen to the announcement, while the ones who were on a call continued to pacify their customers.

"New guy on the floor. My trainee. First day. First sale," she summarised.

Every one clapped. The guys, who were on calls clapped too, without even listening to what Sushmita had said. She glanced at me.

"You made me proud," she said.

"Oh, it's just part of the pridification I initiated." I winked at her.

• • •

It was three. I had gone back to calling after my first sale, hoping I would be able to push another one in, but unfortunately I had to settle with one for the day. As I gathered my belongings to get back to our room and crash, Sushmita came up to me.

"Hey, I owe you a treat. Do you want to go get a drink?" she asked.

"Oh, are you asking me out?" I asked, in a flirty tone.

"No, technically I am asking you IN," she said.

"Care to explain?"

"It's 3 in the morning kiddo. All the pubs are closed. I was asking if you want to come TO my HOUSE for a drink."

"That sounds exciting. But I don't drink," I said, with an innocent face.

"You will. Today." She ordered.

"No way."

"You will," she said and turned around to leave.

"See you in the car parking," she shouted as she walked away.

I was sure I wouldn't drink. But I wasn't too sure if I could keep myself from kissing her. I just decided to do what my heart wanted me to and see where it took us, as she had told me before. I scurried towards the car parking after letting Rohit know that I wouldn't be going back to our PG with him. He punched my stomach and pulled my leg a few times before letting me go. Sushmita stood leaning against her Black Maruthi Swift, waiting for me, with a cigarette in her hand.

"Are you smoking weed again?" I asked as I walked up to her.

"Nope. It's just some tobacco mixed with tar and nicotine," she said.

"Wanna drive?" she asked, throwing me the key.

I caught the key, shrugged and occupied the extra-cushioned seat behind the wheel. Sushmita dropped her cigarette and slipped into the car, throwing her bag in the back seat.

"I am going to keep the windows down. I need some fresh air," I said.

"You just stole the words from my mouth," she said and laughed.

I glanced at her. She looked tired yet entrancing. Psychiatrists could use her to hypnotise me. I didn't want to steal words from her mouth. I wanted to steal her lips. I glanced at them. They were dry but had the words 'kiss me' written all over them. I slowly leaned towards her, and as I did, I accidentally placed my hand on the horn. The sound startled me. She laughed.

But why? Did she know I was going to kiss her? Or did she just laugh because of my reaction to the horn? I glanced at her again.

"Do you have a starting problem?" she asked, snapping her fingers.

She finally woke me up from my hypnotic state.

"What?" I asked.

She repeated her question. I sensed a second meaning in that line.

No, I can start well and finish well too. I wanted to tell her.

"No, I-I am just trying to adjust my seat," I said.

She laughed again. The more she laughed, the harder it was for my lips to hold back their enthusiasm. I controlled myself, started the car and drove out of the parking lot.

• • •

We stepped into her apartment on the second floor of a three-storey building. My eyes wandered around her house in default, as soon as she turned the lights on.

It was a cute single bedroom apartment. There was a large 35-inch LED TV fixed on the wall of the living room and a white couch a few meters away from it. There was a coffee table beside the couch. The area between the TV and the couch was occupied by a fluffy black carpet. The bedroom was on the right and the kitchen on the left. The living room was large and had more than enough space for a four-seater dining table. Although Sushmita had hectic work schedules, she managed to keep her house flawlessly tidy.

"I like your couch," I said and sat on it.

"Me too. This is where I pass out when I get home drunk," she said.

I smiled and folded up my shirt sleeves.

"Wait. I'll fix us drinks," she said and walked away in a hurry.

"I don't drink," I reminded her.

She neither listened to what I said nor bothered to reply. She came back with two glasses of liquor with some ice cubes in them and shoved one of them into my hand.

"What's this?" I asked.

"Whisky. On the rocks. I like it this way."

"I don't drink," I said again, stressing on my words to make it clear.

She did not bother again. "Cheers," she said and tapped my glass.

She took a sip. I inhaled the smell of the spirit and placed the glass aside. She laughed.

“Since when have you been drinking?” I asked. “Four years,” she said.

“How old are you?”

She raised an eyebrow as though I was asking for her Facebook password.

“I am a couple of years older than you,” she said, in a blunt tone.

“How do you know my age?” I asked, placing my feet on the coffee table, trying to make myself comfortable.

“That information was on your resume, kiddo.” She laughed again and brushed my hair.

That laugh tormented my senses.

“Stop laughing. You urge me to kiss you,” I said. Yes, I had to tell it to her. I couldn’t take it anymore.

Her eyes paralysed mine as they met. I couldn’t even blink. She gulped down the whisky like a pro and placed the glass on the table. She leaned back on the couch.

She smiled.

“Drink,” she said, pointing at my glass.

“No. I am good.”

She turned her head towards me. There was something different in her eyes. They were larger, dilated, inviting and captivating and what not. She stood up and picked up the glass of whisky. She moved closer to me.

My heart began to jump like a fish out of water. She seductively sat on my lap and put her arm around my shoulders. My manhood began to react. I put my arm around her waist. She held the glass beside my mouth and brought her lips close to my ears.

“Drink,” she whispered, in a magnetic tone.

I just could not react. My body was numb. The smell of her perfume arrested me. She took the glass away from my lips and emptied its contents into her mouth. She held me firmly by my cheeks and placed her lips on mine.

She transferred all the whisky from her mouth into mine. I closed my eyes and gulped it down, surrendering to her.

The concentration of the spirit burned my mouth and chest, making me squawk. She transferred a piece of half melted ice into my mouth, using her tongue and swirled it around the inside, cooling down the burning sensation. She continued to kiss me. She adjusted herself, putting her legs on either side of me, as we worked our lips over each other. I put my hands inside her shirt and held her bare hips as my manhood poked her, asking her questions.

She unbuttoned the first few buttons of my shirt and slipped her long fingers through it. She made irregular circles on my chest as the kissing got deeper and more passionate. I moved my hands towards her stomach and began to unbutton her shirt from inside. I broke the kiss, opened her shirt and kissed the back of her neck. She leaned forward and bit my ear, then ran her tongue around it, tickling me in the process.

"Let's go to the bedroom," she whispered into my ear.

I stood up and walked towards the bedroom, carrying her, her legs clinging to either side of my waist. I placed her on the bed and climbed over her. A few drops of her sweat trickled down her neck and disappeared into her breasts. Her stomach shivered under me, as her breathing got heavier. She pulled me closer to her, as every strand of hair on my body stood up in lust. Our bare stomachs pushed against each other with every gasp of breath we took. I rolled her R, kissed her W and bit her V. She moaned and squealed for the rest of the night, digging her fingernails into my back as I entered the depths of desire.

By the time I collapsed on her, day had almost broken. Our clothes were fast asleep on the floor. There were a few hickies around her neck and a few scratch marks on my back. We were sweating all over and gasping for breath.

"This was amazing," she said and softly pecked my cheek.

"You are a beast," I said, my nostrils still searching for oxygen.

She lifted her head and attempted to bite my cheek. I moved my head away in the nick of time and sat up, facing a dressing table mirror. I turned around and looked at my back in the mirror to see the scratch marks.

"Looks like you finally scratched my back," I said and winked at her.

"You want more of those?" she asked, in a seductive tone.

"I am tired," I said, with my lower lip stuck out, inviting her to pamper me.

"You are such a girl," she said.

"Well, I've shown you biological proof that I am not," I teased.

"Is it? I don't remember. I guess I will have to test your documents again," she said, winking.

"You are definitely asking me IN, aren't you?" I laughed and moved closer to her.

• • •

A Year Later

"Rohit. Where is Sushmita?" I asked, walking towards his cabin.

"I don't know, *da*. Did you check the smoking zone?" he asked.

"Yes. Let me try the car parking," I said.

"Aren't you coming with me?" he asked as I started to walk away.

"No, *da*. I'll take the office cab or something."

Our shift was over, and we were supposed to be heading back to our PG. Rohit was quite used to going back alone, as he knew I liked to spend time with Sushmita after our shifts.

It had been precisely a year since our hearts and skin first felt the warmth of each other.

From an interviewer to a trainer, to a colleague, to a friend, to a friend with benefits, to a relationship that was still rummaging through different words in the English dictionary to christen itself, she found her way deeper and deeper into me.

Although my very first day on the call floor won me applause and an unforgettable treat at Sushmita's house, the days that followed were horrible. I sucked at sales. I scraped through my sales target thanks to the constant support I got from Sushmita and Rohit.

In this one year, the number of mobile phone connections I sold was much lesser than the number of kisses I sold to Sushmita. She had stopped calling me kiddo. She used words like 'baby', 'shona' and 'sweetheart' instead. I finally replaced Shruthi's picture in my mobile phone wallpaper, with a picture collage of Mohanlal, Kamal Haasan and Aamir Khan.

"The solution to losing a girl is finding another one," Sushmita used to say, during the rare occasions I spoke about Shruthi.

"Will you be the girl I am dying to find?" I asked on one of those occasions.

She remained silent. I never knew what was going through her mind. I knew she liked me a lot. I could feel the magical connect our hearts had. There were times when we spent several hours together without even having a conversation and still felt good about being with each other. But somehow she was never ready to discuss commitment and a full life together. Nevertheless, I made sure I cherished every moment I spent with her, fearing that it would all come to an end one fine day.

I reached the car parking area and found her right beside her car. She was dressed in a green saree with floral designs draped in Bengali style.

"Do you have any clue how beautiful you look today?" I asked.

I had already complimented her at least a hundred times during our shift, but I still couldn't stop. I couldn't take my eyes off her the entire day. There was something about the saree that made my eyeballs follow her, like a mariner's compass.

She raised her hand, gesturing for me to be silent as she was on a call. She hung up and faced me. Her lips widened, expressing a mixed emotion of a blush and a triumphant grin.

"Mr. Sengupta. My ex," she said.

My smile dropped sending 'answer-in-detail' questions to my brain.

"What does he want?" I asked while the vein in my temple protruded as I gnashed my teeth.

"It's been two years now since we parted. He called to wish me for the anniversary and asked me the same question he asked last year."

"I hope you are okay." I was concerned.

"Yes. I told him the number of guys I slept with after the divorce."

"How many?" I asked, reflexively.

"One," she said and slapped my elbow.

"You could have told him how many times too," I said, with a wink.

"I'll save that answer for next year."

"Does that mean I have a year's extension?" I asked, with an innocent face.

She turned quiet all of a sudden. She looked away to avoid the awkwardness of the sudden silence.

"It is a beautiful night. Isn't it?" she said.

She was so used to the 'answer-any-eight-out-of-ten-questions' type question paper format. In my case, she had the liberty to choose the number of questions she wanted to answer.

"Yes. It is."

I made sure I attended all her questions. I always yearned for full marks with her. It indeed was a pleasant night. The breeze was gentle and passionate. I liked the way it softly played with her hair and refreshed her skin. At times, it got a little naughty, blowing away her saree around her navel.

"I want to ride pillion with you on a bike," she said with an adorable face.

I liked the idea. But I had no bike.

"No bike," I said.

"Can you ask Rohit?" she said.

"Only if he is allowed to sleep on his office table wearing boxers," I said.

She laughed. I was still addicted to her laugh. She looked at me the way I had looked at my parents as a kid, whenever I wanted something.

"Wait. I'll make him an offer he can't refuse," I said, in Marlon Brando style.

"Which is?"

"Give me your car keys."

• • •

We rode through the lonely roads of Bangalore at half-past-three in the morning. The wind was cold and blissful. Sushmita had her hand around my waist holding my stomach. She sat with both legs on one side and rested her chin on my shoulder. The cold wind just couldn't beat the warmth of her breath behind my ear.

"I just don't want to hurt you, *shona*," she said.

It took a moment for me to understand that she was answering the question I had asked her earlier. She had left some space for difficult questions in the answer paper, to come back and answer later.

"Why would you?" I asked.

"I don't know. This whole commitment thing is just not my cup of tea. I am really not able to tune myself into it. My parents forced me into marriage. He was a rich businessman's son. His wealth made my parents overlook his character. They didn't even try to find out.

I was not his first wife. He was married to someone else, who had apparently committed suicide due to depression. He hardly came home after we got married. He was on constant business trips. But when he came home, life was hell. My senses have become stale ever since our divorce. I just don't want to follow a pattern in life. I am simply picking the things that keep me happy. I really love you, sweetheart. But I don't want to give you hopes of a normal married life together. If you ever feel you should let go of this complication for a clear life ahead, I wouldn't hold you back."

I felt wetness on my shoulder. She was crying. I really didn't know what to say. Nor did I know what to say to console her. I was forced to remain silent because I knew I had to choose the right words to pacify her. A few more drops fell on my shoulder and then on my face and arms. I looked up. It had begun to rain. She pulled herself closer to me. I felt her fingers shiver on my stomach. She rested her cheek on my shoulder and hugged me tightly.

I could feel how much she wanted me. But the whole scenario confused me. I wasn't sure where I was heading. I did not have a clear picture of a future between us. I had tears in my eyes. I knew she was still crying too. I decided to keep riding and let the rain do the arduous task of washing away our tears.

The rain got heavier in some time. I could not ride properly as I did not have a helmet on. We stopped under a tree and got off the bike. The both of us observed each other's silence. I wanted to run the entire storyline in my mind before I came up with a clear decision. I knew she was trying to figure out what was running through my mind. She looked at me. I looked away and set my eyes on the road. The damaged road allowed the rain to form puddles.

Sushmita had a damaged life, and I didn't want any more puddles in her journey. I was selfish, unlike her. She was okay with me leaving her. But I just couldn't get enough of the love she had for me. Some relationships work. Some don't. They crash even after marriage. I had a live example standing before me. It was all about how long our hearts decided to travel with each other.

Marriage is an eyewash to society. It is an algorithm that our ancestors programmed into our brains. A senseless bond that ties you up as a couple in society, even if you have lost your love for each other.

After Shruthi left, I had no plans of getting married anyway. I just wanted to get into films and lead the life of an actor. A wedding was not planned in my cards at all. So, why would I even have to think of leaving Sushmita? Why couldn't I be with her as long as our hearts sang the same melody? Why shouldn't we be the real human beings, the animals that god intended to make out of us?

"Can you handle rumours?" I asked, finally breaking the silence.

"What?" she asked, confused.

"I will turn into a celebrity soon. The press will write a lot about us as we wouldn't be a married couple. Can you handle that?" I asked, smiling at her.

"Only if you let me walk the red carpet with you," she said, blushing to glory.

I laughed and stepped closer to her. I held her hand and went on my knee.

"No engagement ring. No *mangalsutra*. No expensive wedding. No bachelor party. No bachelorette party.

No honeymoon. No children. No family planning. No commitments. No restrictions. Just our hearts full of love and our heads full of understanding. Will you NOT marry me Sushmita?"

I hadn't seen her blush so much ever before. I could see chills running through every nerve in her body. Her exasperation just did not let her speak. She looked at me with tears that were visible, in spite of the rain.

"Forever, Abi," she said.

I blushed and got to my feet. The rain had washed away all the question marks that we drew on us. She suddenly appeared clear and more beautiful. I looked at her. Her saree kissed her body, enhancing her enticing curves. The water droplets on her face and eyelashes looked like fresh dew from the early morning grass. Her wet hair drove me crazy.

"I want to kiss you now," I said.

"Those are my lines. Give it back," she said.

I grabbed her by her hip and pulled her closer to me. I pushed my fingers into her wet hair, as my lips sucked up the drops of water on her lips. We kissed hard. There was more passion in it than ever before. May be it was because we were finally clear on what roles we were playing.

"Your clothes are wet, baby. You need to be undressed," she said.

"So are yours," I said.

"Let's get home."

• • •

"It's a weekend. Why are you still glued to your laptop?" I asked Rohit.

We were in our room on a lazy Saturday afternoon. Rohit was still working, while I lay down on my bed with my legs raised high, rested on the wall.

"Appraisal time, buddy. Work's endless," he said, still staring at his laptop.

"How is my score?" I asked.

"Average."

"Thank god. At least I am not in the 'poor' list."

"You would have been if you had not made that bulk sale," he said.

I was lucky I rung into a Malayali's house in the UK. It was generally difficult to sell anything to an Indian living abroad. Moreover, we were dealing with stuff that people could just buy from the market without risking giving their credit card numbers to an anonymous sales person, with a pseudo name. I spoke to the Malayali customer in Malayalam, breaking the QC norms. He felt comfortable with me and gave me plenty of references. I used the reference numbers and made twenty-four sales in ten days, which was more than two times my sales target.

Rohit helped me pass the quality check, considering the number of sales it brought to the company.

"You might be promoted to senior customer service representative this year," he said.

"I don't care. I am just working for my parents," I said.

"And I am just doing my work," he said, with a smirk.

My phone buzzed before I could respond to him.

"Hello," I said, lazily.

"Abhishek Krishnan?"

"This is him."

"I am Sanjay calling from Top Notch Entertainment.

We are a startup production house."

"Uh-huh." I was so used to responding like that after talking to UK customers for a year.

"We are on the verge of making a romcom. Your pictures grabbed our attention," he said.

I was not excited at all. I had received so many similar calls in the past one year, and nobody seemed legitimate.

"I'm glad," I said, with absolutely no feeling of gladness.

"Can we meet for a quick chat?"

"Sure. Why not?" I said.

"5 p.m. Indira Nagar Coffee day?"

"Sounds good to me," I said and hung up.

The guy seemed professional. Our conversation was in English, which meant he was educated too, unlike the useless morons I met before. However, I wasn't excited yet.

• • •

My conversation with Sanjay lasted for an hour. He was an MBA in media management and was working as the operations manager of Top Notch Entertainment.

"Although we are a startup, we are well-funded," Sanjay said.

"Where is your office?" I asked.

"Bangalore. We are setting one up in Chennai too at the moment," he said.

"Okay. What are you offering me?" I asked.

"Well, this is about a typical love triangle. We are looking at some of the top actors for the male and female lead. But the director feels you will perfectly fit the second lead."

I did nothing but smile.

"Hmmm. So what next?" My questions were plain, simple and straightforward.

"We will have a screen test next Saturday. The director is coming down. We are taking this nice and easy. We don't want to rush into things. We've got the funds. We've got a good story. We just want to make the best out of it."

"Do you expect me to pay you anything?" I asked, frankly.

He laughed.

"Why would we do that? It's usually the other way around, right? Or has the industry changed in the two years I was away doing my masters?"

I laughed.

"It's a crazy world out there, buddy. You have no clue."

"I'd better be cautious then. Alright. See you next Saturday. I'll give you a call or drop you a line," he said.

"Sure."

We shook hands. A handshake of hope that leaked out through tiny cracks in the wall I built, exactly thirteen months ago. But I still kept my enthusiasm down. I knew it wasn't time to rejoice yet.

• • •

"That was amazing, Abhishek," Sanjay lauded.

I was at the screen test. The director had asked me to enact a love failure scene. The director's name was Jithin, a young man, who had a lot of experience in the advertising field. He appeared to be clear about what he wanted.

I really liked the office. It was spacious and designed in style with contemporary furniture and wall paintings.

"Thank you," I said, with a grin.

It had been a really long time since I was complimented for my acting skills and it felt good to come back. A lot had happened in showbiz during my downtime.

Daniel, the chap who acted with me in the serial, had a strong fan base because of his performance in the Tamil movie, *Idharkudhaane Aasaipattai Balakumara*.

Rajan P Dev sir, whom I acted with, in the same serial, had passed away due to liver disease. Sreedev, my classmate back in college, was acting in a Malayalam serial for Surya TV. I thought it was time for me to make some news too.

"Okay, Abhishek. So here is the deal," Jithin said. "We will roll in two months. The schedule is going to be long. We will be shooting for a good six months with tiny breaks in between. Most of your portions will be shot in London."

Wow! I told myself.

"Stop shaving from today. I would love a two-month old beard on your face. It would also be great if you bring some shape to your body. At least, some visible biceps because you will be playing a gym trainer."

He gave me a moment to swallow his demands. "Deal?" he asked.

"Double deal," I said.

"Superb."

"Ummmm. Do I have to pay you anything?" I asked, again.

I wanted to be doubly sure that there were no strings attached. Jithin glanced at Sanjay to check if he had asked for money. Sanjay shrugged.

"Pay? You mean for the travel?" Jithin asked, confused.

"He asked me the same question the other day," Sanjay said.

"Yes. You know, I've gone through so much shit dealing with the wrong people. I am just clearing my doubts before I get excited," I said.

Jithin laughed. "I understand, buddy. There is no way we can trouble you. Don't worry. We are doing this."

He held his fist up for a fist bump. I acknowledged. I finally permitted my heart to rejoice.

• • •

"I guess I should put in my papers," I told Sushmita and Rohit.

We were at the smoking zone at our office.

"When is the shoot commencing?" Rohit asked.

"In a couple of months. So, if I give my resignation letter now, my notice period will be served before the shoot starts."

"Can't you just go on leave?" Sushmita asked.

"We will be shooting for six months. They wouldn't give me leave for half a year."

"That's right. Where are you shooting?" Rohit asked.

"London."

Sushmita's eyes lit up.

"I am in," she told Rohit and hugged me.

"What is happening?" I asked, genuinely confused.

"We have a new process coming in. Sushmita is one among the few, who are selected to go to London and undergo training for six months," Rohit said.

"I was not sure if I wanted to go. Now I don't want to let go of this opportunity," she said.

"I didn't know that heights of coincidence could crawl up to the seventh floor of this building," I said.

"I am so excited. Come let's go get drunk," she said.

"It's just dinner break on Monday, and we are still struggling to hit our target. Let's get to work." The production manager inside Rohit poked his head out.

We laughed and walked in.

• • •

I mailed my resignation letter to my operations manager and the HR, giving them the real reason and also requested them for permission to have a beard during my notice period. I just had to serve a month's notice period as I was resigning as a junior customer service representative. My beard grew along with my biceps. I was working hard to do justice to the character that director Jithin had in mind. I distributed sweets to my colleagues on my last day at work.

"Don't forget me when you become a star," one of them said.

"I'll do my best, buddy," I joked.

I really didn't know why people said that. Do people get struck with amnesia when they are over-exposed to the camera and lights? I thought it was a silly thing to say. Nevertheless, things were finally falling into place. I was walking out of a corporate to continue from where I had left off.

• • •

19

Best Outgoing Student

Chalu and I tiptoed into our department, trying to sneak into class before getting noticed. We were late again as Chalu was suddenly curious to find out the number of strands in his moustache. We left as soon as he gave up.

"Abi." Someone called from behind us. It was Ilamparithi sir.

"Congrats," he said.

Was he lauding me for being the most consistent latecomer in the history of Masan Memorial College?

"Sorry, sir. The alarm didn't go off," I said, like a preprogrammed robot.

"That's okay. It's your time now," he said. I gave him a confused look.

"You have won the best outgoing student award." He dissolved my confusion.

"Thanks sir."

I wasn't too excited as they had already hinted that I had won by a decent margin. Moreover, I was missing Shruthi. I just wanted her to come back. I wanted to help her come out of whatever she was going through.

"How is your serial shaping up?" Ilamparithi sir asked.

"The next schedule is soon, after the channel approves the pilot episodes."

"Can't wait, Abi. I am happy for you. You are slowly stepping into the professional arena. Work hard, stay ethical and be punctual."

He glanced at Chalu as he said that.

"Buy a new alarm clock and stay away from Chalu." He winked.

I chuckled. Chalu gave him a wide grin and fiddled with his moustache, not knowing what to say.

"Okay, sir. I've got some editing work to finish," I said and hurried into the television production lab before Chalu had ideas of going back to counting his moustache.

• • •

THE NEXT DAY

Although I wasn't too excited about being announced the best outgoing student, the exaggerated excitement of my friends cost me fourteen bottles of beer and a couple of plates of chicken biriyani. As we lined up the bottles of beer on Chalu's terrace in a mood to exploit every inch of the open space, my phone vibrated in my pocket.

My mind gathered a visual of Shruthi, dressed in white, holding her phone to her ear, waiting for me to answer her call. I slipped my fingers into my pocket intensely hoping it was her. I was longing to hear her voice.

My heart vibrated along with my phone when the caller ID displayed her name along with a picture of her smiling at me erasing all my worries.

"You have no clue of how much I waited for this moment," I said, not bothering to use the first words Alexander Grahambell used when he invented the telephone.

"I want to meet you, Abi." She sounded worried.

"I am dying to," I said.

"Can you to come to Marrybrown at Anna Nagar now?"

"I am on my way," I said and slid down the stairs after assuring the others that I would be back soon.

• • •

I observed the neat interiors of Marrybrown through its glass walls as I parked my bike outside. She was already there. She was wearing a plain yellow T-shirt that proudly sat on her incredible body. I adjusted my hair using the rearview mirror and unbuttoned the first button of my shirt. She liked it that way, and I wanted to look good for her.

I walked in and sat on the chair opposite her. She was staring at the table with her chin rested on her hand.

"Hi," I said.

She looked up at me. Her face was absolutely pale. There was no *kajal* in her eyes, *bindi* on her forehead or the adorably attractive smile on her lips. Her hair was left loose and not combed properly.

"Hi," she said, her voice not reaching my ears entirely.

Something was very wrong. I couldn't bear seeing her this worried. Her eyeballs moved around as she surveyed my face. They kept scanning every inch of my face and soon drowned in a well of tears. My heart picked up a spade and dug through my chest in an attempt to jump out.

I held both her hands with both of mine. They were shivering. She clenched my hands tightly as a few drops of her tears fell on them.

"What's wrong, baby?" My voice broke.

The tears started flowing out uncontrollably, drenching my hands. She placed her forehead on them and began to weep. I felt miserable. I attempted to lift her head. But she didn't want to. I looked around. People were staring at us.

"Let's go somewhere else," I said and lifted her by her hand.

"No. You go, Abi. I'll call you," she said.

The last thing I wanted to do was to leave her when she was upset.

"Shruthi, I can't leave you like this. I want you to talk to me. I want to see you smile before I go."

She wiped her tears and looked up at me.

"I can't talk now, Abi. I just can't. Please go back home. I'll call you. I promise."

"Why not now?" I asked.

"You will know when I call you," she said.

I was confused. I frowned at her. She looked away for a moment and then looked at me.

"Go. I'll call you as soon as you get home," she said.

I gave her a close look. Something was definitely wrong. But why was she reluctant to tell me right there? I knew well that she wouldn't ask me to do something without a justified reason behind it.

Was someone watching us? I quickly looked around to check if her dad or someone else was around. I decided to do exactly what she said.

"Okay. I am going. I'll call you as soon as I get home," I said and walked away reluctantly.

She needed me for sure. I couldn't wait to get home.

• • •

I put my hand on my mobile inside my pocket every now and then, as I rode back anticipating her call. I went straight to Chalu's house and entered his room. I did not want to go to the terrace as I was not sure if I had to discuss this with my friends yet. I took my mobile out to find that there was a message from her already, which I had failed to catch on my way back. My thumb shivered as it hit the OPEN button. It was a long message.

"Abi. I love you so very much, and I know exactly how much you love me. You make me feel like the flowers that bloom after a morning shower of rain. But Abi my petals are losing their fragrance. I don't think I deserve you. I really don't know how to say this. Things are not happening as expected. I think we should part ways. I wanted to tell this to you in person. But when I look at your face, I am reminded of all the wonderful things we did together. I guess we won't see each other again. I know I have drowned you in a rain of tears. But I am helpless, Abi.

Life is like these dark grey passing clouds. Just let them rain down and carry on with life. I am one of those passing clouds, Abi. Please forgive and forget me. Consider me a dark patch of your past. I love you, Abi and I'll miss you like crazy. But I am going to have to let go of your hand. I want to see you shine as a successful actor. Remember I will always be watching you from far far away. I am terribly sorry for coming into your life. Will love you forever. Goodbye."

My vision blurred with the tears that showed up after I read the first few lines. I couldn't read further. I did not want to believe what I read. I called her. Her phone was switched off. I called her again. Switched off. I called her again and again and again. I redialled her number like crazy. I was out of my mind.

How could she do this to me? What was she hiding from me? Why didn't I have the privilege to know? How could I live without her? How could she live without me?

My heart was exploding as my mind repeated these questions in a never-ending loop. I couldn't hold myself together. I sat on the floor and began weeping. The rains that she mentioned showed up in my eyes. It was heavy. It was terrible. It was heart-aching. I did not have the strength to stand up. I just lay on the floor and dialed her number repeatedly in a ridiculously desperate attempt to hear her voice.

I cursed myself for leaving her just because she asked me to. I did not know that I was walking away from her life. I wanted to meet her. I knew I could change her mind. I knew I could get her out of the mess she was in. I knew I could make her un-type the message she had sent. I wanted her that very moment. I really did.

• • •

I composed myself and searched for my bike key after having heard the recorded voice that said *'the number you are calling is currently switched off'* a zillion times. As I began to leave, teary-eyed, completely out of my mind, Chalu walked into his room.

"What happened?" he asked, the small beer buzz leaving his head as soon as he saw my state.

I had no choice but to explain to him what had happened. "I am going with you to meet her," he said.

"Come," I said.

I wasn't too sure if I could deal with the scenario myself. It was drizzling outside. Chalu decided to take his car.

"You drive. I am drunk," he said.

I drove as fast as possible, ignoring the drizzle, the traffic, my driving inexperience and every other obstacle that came my way. I reached her house. There was a truck waiting inside her compound, and the entire area smelled of coffee. I overlooked everything, ran inside and rang the doorbell. The door opened almost immediately. She stood before me as shattered and messy as I was. Her red eyes and swollen face explained to me that she had been crying.

"What's wrong, Shruthi?" I asked.

"I messaged you. It is over," she said, looking away.

"You don't mean it, Shruthi," I said.

"I have no choice."

She turned around and walked into her house. I followed her and held her hand.

"Please leave, Abi. My dad will be here any moment."

"I don't care. Give me an answer," I said.

"Please don't ask me anything. I don't know the answer to your questions. All I know is this is not working, and we have to end this here before we hurt each other more."

"You've already hurt me. It can't get worse. Why did you even come into my life if you wanted to abandon me halfway?" I had no clue if I was using the right words.

She turned and looked at me. Her eyes couldn't withstand her overflowing flood of tears.

"Yes. It is my mistake. I shouldn't have come into your life. I shouldn't have given you hopes of a life together. I am a heartless wreck. I have done nothing but hurt every person around me. I do not want anyone anymore."

She began to weep. I couldn't see her cry. It had always been my biggest weakness. I really did not know why all this was happening to us. Was it because of something I did that she was breaking up? I tried to recollect the little things that she was unhappy about in the past. There was nothing unforgivable that came to my mind.

"Is it because of me that you are breaking up with me? Did I do anything wrong?" I asked.

She did not answer. She just kept weeping. I stepped forward and held her hand.

"Tell me, Shruthi. Have I done anything wrong?"

I held her hand and forced her to slap me left and right continuously.

"Hit me. Kill me. But please don't say that you are leaving me." I turned psychotic with all the pain and confusion.

She forcefully took her hand away and hugged me. She exploded into tears as she collapsed on me.

"I don't want to do this, Abi. But I have to. Please don't ask me anything else. I don't deserve you. I am sorry for all that happened. Please leave." She gently pushed me away and ran inwards.

"SHRUTHI," I shouted from behind her and attempted to go after her.

I was stopped by a voice that startled all of us. It was her dad.

"What's happening here?" he asked, in a loud and angry voice.

Shruthi quickly turned around to face her dad.

"*Appa*. It's nothing. We are just solving an issue," she said, trying endlessly to wipe away her tears.

"Uncle, I love Shruthi. I want her in..."

"Leave right now or I'll call the police," he said, before I could complete what I wanted to say. His voice grew louder and sterner.

"Uncle. Please. Listen to..."

"Another word and I will file a complaint that you are harassing my daughter." He took his mobile out and threatened me.

I looked at Shruthi. She appeared helpless. Chalu held my hand and dragged me outside.

"Come, *da*. Listen to me," he said.

I had my eyes fixed on Shruthi as Chalu pulled me out through the open door. She stared at me, and before we could have enough eye contact, her dad shut the door with a loud bang.

It was pouring outside. Chalu ran towards his car and got into the driver's seat. He opened the door for me to get in. I kicked it shut and walked. I took a few steps forward and collapsed on my knees, crying uncontrollably, succumbing myself to the showers of despair.

20

Moving in with Sushmita

"Sush, do you think I should move into your house," I asked.

I was lying on her couch, resting my head on her lap. She was reading a book, while I was fiddling with her iPad.

"Yes *shona*, I was thinking of that too. But let's just finish our schedules in London first," she said.

"It's my birthday next week. I think I should throw you guys a party."

"Who all?" she asked.

"Rohit and you. And also probably that cute receptionist."

She pinched my ear.

"Don't call her cute. She has a name."

"Ouch!" I winced in pain.

"Invite her to the party. I will make sure I dress better than her, and you won't take your eyes off me," she said.

I glanced at her face from the low angle of her lap.

"You look incredibly adorable when you are jealous," I said and pulled her cheek.

"Don't try to pacify me. You have done the damage already," she said, pretending to be angry.

"Are you inviting me for a kiss?"

"You wish," she said and continued to read her book.

I casually glanced at her iPad and noticed something that caught my attention. It was a news article in Behindwoods – a web portal for Tamil cinema.

AD FILMMAKER JITHIN NAMBIAR TO DIRECT A ROMCOM

By Kaushik L.M | Jan 3, 2014

Ad film director Jithin Nambiar, who gave us many interesting commercials, is now venturing into K-town.

The movie is said to be a romantic comedy that will have top names in the industry playing the lead pair.

The film will be a high-budget affair set mostly in London and will be produced by Top Notch Entertainment. It is said that the director has been approaching big names for the music and camera departments. Debut actor Ashish Punja will play the second lead in the film.

Stay tuned for more updates.

I was shocked to read the article. I read the name Ashish Punja over and over again, until I was convinced that it was not Abhishek Krishnan. My hands began to shake. I quickly got up and called Sanjay.

"Hello."

"Sanjay?"

"Yes."

"Sanjay. Abhishek here."

"Yup. I have your number, man," he said.

"I just read an article in Behindwoods. It says Ashish Punja is playing the second lead. Is this true?"

"Yeah, man. The producer wants to cast his son. Jithin is not happy with him at all. He is a bad actor."

"But I have been working my ass off, Sanjay. You should have told me."

"I understand, Abhishek. I am sorry man. I was going to call you one of these days. The guys at Behindwoods are way too quick with movie updates. You know how it is here. The producer's word is final. We did our best to rope you in. You were right. It's a crazy world out here. I promise we'll work something out for you next time."

I hung up without saying another word. Tears flooded my eyes. I began to weep. Sushmita was shocked by my sudden breakdown.

"What happened?" she asked.

I showed her the news article. She was dismayed reading it. She held me close to her. She had tears in her eyes too.

I hugged her and cried. My dream of acting in movies, my excitement of staying with Sushmita in London, my job, my hard work—they were all torn to bits.

"Why me, Sush? Why me always?"

"Don't cry, sweetheart. Let's just let this time pass quickly." She caressed my hair and kissed my forehead as I continued to cry. I soon collapsed in her lap and held her hand tightly. She continued to caress my hair until I fell asleep.

• • •

I woke up after a couple of hours. It was four in the evening. I found myself in Sushmita's bedroom and heard the sound of porcelain in the kitchen. Sushmita walked towards the bedroom sipping coffee.

"Awake so soon? Want some coffee?" she asked.

I looked at her for a while. She was wearing a loose T-shirt and shorts and still looked beautiful.

"Whisky. On the rocks," I said. She looked up at me and smiled.

"Are you sure?" I nodded.

She left and came back in a minute with ice cubes ringing bells inside the glass. She handed the glass to me.

"How did I end up in your bed?" I asked.

"Woman power," she said while showing me her biceps.

Half my lips smiled while the other half was still paralysed after the bad news. I took a few quick sips. Sushmita realised I was still depressed. She sat beside me and placed her hand on my shoulder.

"Baby, I know you've gone through a lot following your passion. But what amazes me is the way you bounce back to normality after every setback and stay focussed on your goal. There hasn't been an instant till date, where you have ever let go of your hope. You are a fighter, *Shona*. I have seen people giving up after a few failures. But the way you cling to your dreams makes me envious. I wish I could be you.

There is never a problem without a solution. It's just that you don't see it because fear, insecurity and lack of passion make you blind. You have neither of the three. Just keep your nerve and believe that time will take you to your destiny. You are already a superstar in my eyes, baby. The world will soon know the same."

"That is a nice dose of pridification, Sush," I said, smiling; this time both the halves widened.

She laughed.

"You know what, honey? I think you should move in one of these days. I suggest you take a break and concentrate on your movies for some time. I will support you. When I come back from London, I am sure you will have some good news for me. And you better walk the red carpet with me," she said.

"I promise," I said and gave her a hug.

My phone buzzed. The call was from an unknown landline number.

"Hello," I said.

"*Macha*. This is Chalu."

"Hiii, *da*. How are you?" I asked, surprised.

It had been quite a while since we spoke, except for the likes and comments we exchanged on our Facebook profiles.

"I am good, *da*. I am in Coimbatore at the moment. I've got something very important to tell you. Can you come down?"

I frowned. "What is it?"

"You come. We'll talk in person," he said.

"Okay. When?" I asked.

"I suggest you start now. Don't bother packing."

"I'll do my best," I said and hung up.

I looked at Sushmita, who looked back at me as bewildered as I was.

• • •

21

The Shocking Truth

Jan 4, 2014

I flew into Coimbatore by 3 p.m. the following day. Sushmita had booked me an afternoon flight. I had insisted she come too, but she had her visa interview the next day. Chalu and Peri were at the airport to receive me. We exchanged buddy hugs. There was a girl beside Peri, who looked very familiar.

"Hi," she said.

"Angelynn, right? Chalu's neighbour?" I asked and glanced at Chalu demanding an explanation.

"Yes. I am glad you remember," she said.

"Peri and Angelynn are dating each other," Chalu said.

"Oh that's nice." I punched Peri's chest.

"You moved to Coimbatore?" I asked Chalu.

"No, my fiancé stays here," he said.

I raised an eyebrow and let out a whistle.

"Ooooh. Fiancé. Interesting. Who is she? Do I know her?"

"Yes, *da*. It's Poornima. The girl I was seeing in college," Chalu said.

"What the... that's freakin' awesome," I said, as I got into the front seat of his car.

Although I sounded excited and happy about meeting my friends after years, I felt there was something that held their exuberances back.

"What's happening, guys? Why are you all so gloomy? All okay?" I asked.

"Let's get home *da*. We'll talk," he said.

• • •

I met Poornima at her house. It was a two-storied house that looked opulent. Her parents were there too. They greeted me and went upstairs after making sure I felt at home. We had lunch along with a few short exchanges of words. I learned that Peri and Chalu had quit their jobs and were on the verge of starting their own design company. They sounded very professional and I was extremely proud of them.

By the time lunch was over, it was 5 p.m. Poornima made strange facial expressions at Chalu, just as we settled down for a chat. She wanted to communicate something to him. Chalu looked at her and nodded as though he already knew what she wanted to tell him.

"Abi, can you come with us? We need to show you something," Chalu said, rising from his seat and putting on his wristwatch.

"Where?" I asked.

"Come," he said.

I was beginning to get impatient. What was all the fuss about?

• • •

Chalu drove through the roads of Coimbatore for about forty minutes. I sat in the front seat and Peri occupied the back seat. They remained silent all the way and the quietness began to create a pressure in my head. Chalu stopped beside a gate.

"Come," he said.

I looked at both of them, confused. We got out of the car. Chalu pushed open the gate. It was old, rusty and creaked loudly as it opened. Chalu and Peri walked in. I followed them. I observed the area around me anxiously. It was a graveyard. Was someone dead? My mind rummaged through all the faces saved in my memory as I walked through the gravestones. I made wild guesses but did not stop at any particular guess, as I could never bear the loss of any of them.

Chalu and Peri suddenly stopped walking. They turned towards a gravestone and looked at me. I took a few steps forward and read the name engraved on the stone.

Shruthi Victor 1988–2011

May your soul rest in peace

I was shaken. My eyes couldn't stop reading the words. I looked at my friends. I was traumatised.

"Are you sure it's her?" I asked as my voice shattered into pieces.

"Yes. It's her," Peri said.

"How?"

"It was a suicide."

My heart burst inside me when I heard that. My hands and legs began to shake. Tears splashed from my eyes.

"Why would she commit suicide?" I asked as the tears began to flow heavily.

"We are still trying to find out, *da*," Chalu said.

I turned around and looked at her grave. "Why, Shruthi? Why did you?" The words fought through, as I struggled for breath because of the weeping.

I knelt down and touched the piece of stone under which she had been lying for the past three years. I put my arms around it.

"Why, baby? Why? Why? Why? Why? Why?" I couldn't stop crying. "You should have called me. I would never have let this happen."

Chalu and Peri sat beside me and held my shoulders. I put my ear on her grave.

"Chalu. She is alive. Her heart is beating. I can hear it." I began to act crazy.

I started digging out the mud around her grave. Chalu tried to stop me. I pushed him away. Both of them held me from behind and dragged me away from her.

"Stop it, Abi," Peri said.

I sat on the floor and continued to cry.

"Let's go, *da*," Chalu said, attempting to pull me up.

I did not budge. I sat right there and cried until my eyes had no tears. Peri and Chalu sat on a bench nearby and just let me cry away all the sorrow.

Memories of our days together flashed through my head. How we first met, the magic smiley, her proposal, the cute little things we did together, the hugs, the kisses, the jokes we shared, the breakup—they all exploded in my mind one after the other.

Why did she leave me? What did she hide from me? I felt horrible for turning around and walking away when she asked me to leave. I should have stayed. I should have been with her. I was sure she was burning on the inside when she asked me to go away. Oh my god. It was all my fault. All these years, I was under the assumption that she was happy and content wherever she was. I was so wrong. I felt horrible. I sat right there on the ground, staring at her grave, motionless.

I slowly stood up after some time and walked aimlessly towards the entrance. I closed the rusty old gate behind me and continued to walk. Chalu and Peri ran after me. I disappeared into the busy streets before they could find me. I walked straight into a bar, where I found Renjith, who took me to his house. I passed out there after a long conversation.

• • •

22

The Sketch

Jan 5, 2014

I woke up by about 11 in the morning the next day. I had a terrible headache as a result of the crying and the liquor. I opened my eyes to find a group of people around me—Chalu, Peri, Renjith, Jesse, Angelynn and Poornima. They were all sitting around me as though they had come to attend my funeral. I felt awkward looking at their faces.

"You want some tea?" Renjith asked.

"Lemon tea, please?" I asked.

Renjith stood up and walked into the kitchen, while I went into the rest room to refresh myself.

• • •

"Abi, we are trying to find the reason behind Shruthi's suicide," Peri said, as I sat on the bed drinking lemon tea.

"How much do you know?" I asked.

"Not too much. We just know that her dad is in jail now. He had some issues with business."

"Oh," I said, not too shocked by the news. There was no bigger shock than the one I underwent the previous day. "How did you get this news?"

"Nithin told us. He works for NDTV. This was something one of his team mates had covered three years ago," Peri said.

I took another sip of lemon tea and tried to think of a way into this case.

"I am sure this case would have been registered in the police station. Should we get their help? Can we find a policeman who will help us?" I asked.

"I can ask dad. He has influence here," Jesse said.

"Wait, I heard Susheel has been transferred to Coimbatore. Edwin uncle told me," Chalu said.

"Susheel? The guy who tried to fight with us in college?" I asked.

"Yeah. He is a sub-inspector now. We are on pretty good terms these days," he said.

Every one of them had been in constant touch with each other. I seemed to be the only one who had diverted into a whole new world.

Chalu called Susheel and explained the case to him. Susheel said he would check and revert by evening. We decided to spend the day at Renjith's house. I called Sushmita and explained what had happened.

"You should stay with your friends until you feel better, baby," she said.

"Okay. But I wanted to be with you on my birthday," I said.

"I'll come to Coimbatore," she said.

"That would be great. I am staying at Renjith's place. Let me know when you arrive. I'll come and pick you up," I said.

"No. Just send me his address. I'll make it."

"Why?"

"Because I might want to surprise you," she said.

"Okay. I'll send you the address."

"Alright. Love you. Bye," she said and hung up.

• • •

I spent the rest of the day sharing my long story and learning what the other guys were doing.

Nithin – News Reporter, NDTV

Peri – Starting his own design company with Chalu

Chalu – Starting his own design company with Peri

Sreedev – Acting in a TV serial for Surya TV

Renjith – Looking for a story to pitch to his father-in-law and make a movie

Manjunath – Assistant cameraman in Tamil cinema

Prabakaran – Program producer, Suvarna TV

Harish – Runs his own used cars showroom. Aspiring director

Muruganandham – Cameraman for Doordarshan, Andaman

Vivek – Graphic Designer, Prayaag, Bangalore

We had lunch. I had a few phone calls with Sushmita, mom and Rohit. I felt glad that the guys were with me. I would have broken into pieces if they were not around.

In a few hours, Susheel walked into Renjith's house, in his police uniform. He appeared to be a little fitter than he was back in college. But none of that mattered to me. What mattered was the solid information he carried with him.

"Shruthi got married to her dad's business partner's son," he said.

"Vineeth?" I asked, after taking a moment to recollect his name.

"Yes. Vineeth. Apparently, they were in love from school."

"What???" I exclaimed, in disbelief. "That's impossible. We were in love with each other in college."

"You never know, buddy. She might've had been two-timing you. I have seen so many cases," Susheel said, in typical policeman language.

"Hey. Don't you dare speak about Shruthi like that!" I said, attempting to pounce on him.

Chalu and Peri held me back before I could add any more damage to the situation. Susheel appeared composed. He was definitely not the rogue we met in college.

"I understand your anger, Abi. I am just being open about the things happening in the world today. I have no intention of hurting you," he said.

I closed my eyes and composed myself. "Why is her father in jail?" Peri asked.

"Cheating in business," Susheel said. "And harassment."

"Harassment?" I asked.

"Yes. He constantly tortured Shruthi to sign some property documents. He was the reason for her suicide. Her autopsy report says that she had bruises on her body."

"Where does Vineeth stay?" Chalu asked.

"They were in Coimbatore. They shut down the business and moved after Shruthi's death. We have no information about his whereabouts now," Susheel said.

I had had enough. I stood up and walked into the bedroom. I just wanted to return to Bangalore. How could Shruthi cheat on me? I tried to recall the number of times she spoke to me about Vineeth. She offered me his helmet the day I went to her house. That definitely meant that he visited her before I did. But their fathers were business partners. So, it could have also been a casual visit.

My mind flashed to the day I met Vineeth at Spencer's Plaza. Shruthi hugged me and told me she loved me, right in front of him. Why would she do that if she was two-timing me? Moreover, she hated him. She told me that the same day. I felt suspicious. I could smell well-cooked masala in this whole case. I turned around and walked back towards the living room.

"I want to know where Vineeth is," I said.

"Why?" Chalu asked.

"Something's not right about this case. I might get a few answers from him."

"Abi, this case has been closed with the appropriate evidence," Susheel said.

"I am not convinced by the evidence. I know Shruthi much better than any other soul on earth. She wouldn't cheat on me. And she wouldn't commit suicide. I have a strong feeling she was murdered."

"This is ridiculous, Abi. You can't reopen the case with a senseless gut feeling. You have to provide sufficient evidence," Susheel said.

"I don't want to reopen the case. I just want to know where Vineeth is," I said, raising my voice so much that it echoed through the room.

There was silence for a moment.

"Okay. Give me his picture or something. I will try and find out. But remember, I will have to treat this as unofficial," he said.

"Are you asking for a bribe?" I asked.

I was being as cold and frank as he was. Susheel just shook his head, smiled and rose from his chair.

"I've got to go guys. I'll wait for the picture. WhatsApp it to me," he said and walked towards the front door.

He stopped at the door and turned around to face me. "I am not the person you met in college. None of us are. Life changes us, man. Grow up." He opened the door and left.

My friends looked at me as though I was a mentally-disoriented patient, who required medical attention. I couldn't agree more. I had been going through a lot of indefinable pain for the last 48 hours, which made me lose steadiness over my own head.

"How do I find Vineeth's picture?" I asked. Everyone looked at me, as clueless as I was.

"Facebook?" Peri asked. "Do you know his surname?"

I took a moment to think and shook my head in vain. I had not come across any instance where Shruthi had mentioned his second name.

Peri gave up after browsing through hundreds of Facebook profiles with the name Vineeth.

"Hey. He is the guy we met at Spencer's Plaza, right?" Chalu asked.

"Yes," I said.

"I remember his face. I can sketch it."

"You can?" I asked, anxiously.

"I can definitely try," he said.

We quickly dug through the drawers in Renjith's writing table and handed Chalu a few sheets of paper and a pen.

• • •

The sketch was ready in less than an hour. The near accuracy of Vineeth's features in the sketch gave me goosebumps. Thinking of how talented an artist Chalu was, I gave him a hug.

"Spot on, *macha*. Send it to Susheel," I said.

"I haven't installed WhatsApp yet. New phone. You send it," he said.

I saved Susheel's number in my phone and took a picture of the sketch. I scrolled down the names in my WhatsApp list.

Sudha Sunil Susheel Sushmita

I stopped scrolling when I got to Susheel. However, I accidentally sent the picture to Sushmita. She replied immediately.

Sushmita: *Why are you sending me this?*

I began to type a reply when I noticed she was typing another message. I stopped typing and waited.

Sushmita: *BTW. How did you get this picture?*

Me: *Do you know him?*

Sushmita: *Obviously. He is Vineeth Sengupta. My ex.*

Me: *WTF.*

I was thunderstruck. My blood began to boil. My insides felt like an active volcano that could erupt anytime. I could feel my organs beginning to heat up with anger, agony and anxiety. I called her right away. My hands shook as I waited for her to answer my call.

"You serious?" I asked, as soon as we were connected.

"What do you mean? I obviously am," she said.

"Fuckkkkk!" I screamed through the phone.

"What happened?" she asked.

"Too complicated to explain now. I'll call you back," I said and hung up.

I noticed Chalu, Renjith and Peri looking at me. I kicked the bean bag beside me and slammed the phone on it. It bounced off the bag and landed safely on the carpet.

"Bastarrrd!" I shouted and punched the bag mercilessly.

The women ran into the room hearing me scream.

I knew I was giving them a lot of trouble. I sat on the floor and rested my head on the bean bag, panting heavily. I had tears in my eyes. I wanted to find Vineeth and kill him. But how was I going to find him.

My impetuous state just did not let me think. I placed my hands on my head trying to hold back the pieces of my brain that were falling apart. All of a sudden, I sprang to my feet, making the spectators jump along with me. I called Sushmita again. She answered before the first ring was complete.

"When did that bastard call you last?" I barked into the phone.

"Two months ago," she said.

"Do you think the number will still be in your call log?"

"I am not sure. I should check."

"Please do and text me the number if you find it," I said.

I glanced back at my friends. They were absolutely shocked. They stared at me, not daring to bat an eyelid. I explained to them the utterly unanticipated twist.

Sushmita texted soon.

Sushmita: *I cannot find the number. But I remember it was from a landline number with STD code 4864. I memorised the code to make sure I don't answer any more calls from that STD code.*

Me: *Okay. Thank you so much.*

Sushmita: *What's going on? I am concerned.*

I could understand her concern.

Me: *Lots. But don't worry. I am okay. I will talk to you soon.*

Sushmita: *Alright. Please stay calm. Love you.*

Me: *Love you too.*

Google told us that the STD code belonged to Adimaly, Idukki district, Kerala. I closed my eyes and tried to envision what connected Vineeth and Idukki. I revisited the 'college days' rack in my memory. I recollected the day at Spencer's Plaza, where Shruthi told me that they were going to Idukki to finish off with an estate deal.

"Yes. That is where he is. He is in Idukki, at his estate," I said.

"What estate?" Renjith asked.

"Tea? Coffee? Cardamom? I don't know. But he is right there. Right now. Probably screwing the life of another girl. Or just looking at himself in a full-sized mirror and masturbating to glory. I am going for him. Who is coming?"

Peri, Chalu and Renjith looked at each other.

I looked at them, my eyes still wide and crazy.

"Not enough. Call our guys. Whoever can make it. Let's devise a plan," I said.

• • •

23

The Plan

Jan 6, 2014

Nithin, Renjith, Chalu, Peri, Sreedev, Prabakaran, Vivek and I assembled around Renjith's dining table. The others could not make it the next day, but they promised they would come as soon as possible. I had planned a pretty straightforward operation with whatever usable bank of ideas my mind had.

"Listen carefully, guys. Please don't interrupt. I might get confused," I said.

"I am thinking of a sting operation," Nithin said.

Everyone glared at Nithin in disbelief. He still hadn't lost the habit of jumping in front of the gun, when the trigger was pulled.

"Sorry. Continue," he said, simpering.

He hadn't changed one bit. I glanced at him for a moment, my mind trying to recollect what I was going to say.

"No, actually, you tell me what you have in mind. I am a little nervous," I said.

"My idea is simple. Take hidden cameras with us and record all the activity around. It will work as evidence."

"Do we have cameras?" I asked.

"I can arrange as many as you want," he said.

"Perfect," I said and leaned back in my chair.

"Now we will have to find the exact location of the estate," I said.

"Do you recall any instance when Shruthi mentioned it to you?" Vivek asked.

I took more than a moment to think. I squeezed all the juices out of my brain, but could not remember any instance.

"Do you at least know what they majorly cultivated at the estate?" Sreedev asked.

I shook my head. Shruthi had mentioned many estates across Tamil Nadu and Kerala. I just couldn't zero in on the estate at Idukki.

"Yesssss!" Chalu said, punching the table.

All of us shifted our gazes towards Chalu, expecting enlightenment on his sudden change of emotion.

"It's coffee," he said.

"How do you know that?" I asked, looking at him from the corner of my eye.

"Remember we went to her house on the day you broke up? There was a truck outside and the entire place smelled of coffee. They were probably bringing home their last harvest before they sold the estate."

"Did the truck have a name or a label on it?" Nithin asked, excited about the fact that we were getting closer.

"I don't remember," Chalu said, after trying to recollect the picture of the truck.

Nithin thought for a moment.

"What was her father's textile company called?" he asked me.

"V. S. Garments," I said.

"Hmmmm... let's see. V... for... Vineeth. S for Shruthi. They named their business after their children. That's sweet," Nithin said.

I glared at him. He grinned at me.

"What next?" he asked, trying to divert me from his 'sweet' statement.

I thought for a while and stood up as though I was going to conduct a PowerPoint presentation at a board meeting. My mind was clear after the brief discussion. I had a decent plan in my head.

"Okay, guys, listen. Adimaly is a small town. It won't be difficult for us to locate a coffee estate there. And now that we know the probable name of the place, it will be easier for us to track him down. As Nithin suggested, let's do a sting operation."

Nithin gave thumbs up but made sure he did not interrupt or utter a word. He had decided to be a gentleman for some time.

"Can you get the kind of cameras that we can fix on our shirt buttons?" I asked Nithin.

He held his thumbs up again.

"Cool. So all of us will have that fixed on our shirts. It would be nice if we have different angles of footage because we have no clue what we are going to encounter. So, the plan is simple guys. We leave tonight, reach Adimaly early morning tomorrow and start looking for the estate. We get there, catch him, beat the shit out of him if necessary and squeeze whatever information possible. Deal?"

"Let's do it," Sreedev said, all pumped up.

The others agreed too. I knew they felt I was being over-ambitious. But, they wanted to do it for me. They wanted to do anything to make me feel better.

• • •

"We need a dog," I said as we walked towards Jesse's father's Innova.

"What for?" Renjith asked.

"For a possible Plan B," I said.

"We can get Lucy," Renjith said.

"What breed is she?"

"Pug."

I chuckled.

"No. I need a bigger dog. Like a German Shepherd or a Dobermann," I said.

"We can get Scotch. He is a trained Rottweiler," Vivek said.

"Where is he?"

"Our farm house in Palakkad. We can pick him up on the way."

"Perfect," I said.

I took the front seat. The remaining six adjusted themselves in the back seat. The ladies decided to stay back and spend a couple of days together, while we set out to solve this mystery. A solution that would probably justify my inability to understand the pain Shruthi went through.

• • •

24

Idukki

Jan 7, 2014

We reached Idukki just before noon the next day. We picked up the cameras on the way and stopped at Vivek's farmhouse in Palakkad to get Scotch. The drive uphill was tiring and nauseating. It got colder as we drove upward.

We drove past different coffee estates reading every name board that we just could not locate any with the name 'V.S.'. We asked the locals around, but everyone seemed clueless.

It began to get dark, and I began to get nervous. Renjith noticed this.

"Don't worry, da. We'll catch him," he said.

Renjith drove the Innova through every nook and corner of Adimaly. He was definitely tired. I turned around to check the faces of my friends. They were all worn out too, but still held on to their determination or at least pretended to. I felt sorry for them.

"I think you guys should go back," I said.

"Why?" Vivek asked.

"I don't know. I-I I am just troubling you guys."

"Don't talk rubbish. You definitely are not," Peri said.

Renjith stepped on the brake all of a sudden. I turned around quickly to check what went wrong. We had reached a dead end. Renjith pulled the handbrake and rested his head on the steering wheel.

"You take rest *da*. I'll drive," Chalu said.

I had had enough. I got out of the car and screamed at the top of my voice. The others got out too. I began to cry. The guys swarmed around me in an attempt to console me.

"Let's go back. Let's fucckinnn' go back," I screamed.

"No. We are not giving up yet," Sreedev said.

"Where the fuck do we check now? It's dark already," I said, still crying.

"This is not the end of the world, buddy. The sun will shine again tomorrow," Prabakaran said.

"Yes. Let's go find a place to crash for the night. We'll start again early morning tomorrow," Peri said.

These guys were angels. I felt guilty that I had been completely out of touch after we left college. They were always available. All I had to do was pick up my phone and call them. There had been instances where they attempted to call me. But I was either busy or felt too low to talk. I did not want to let them know that I was struggling. It was my stupid inferiority complex, and I hated myself for it.

We spent a few minutes at the dead end to loosen our muscles. Vivek took Scotch for a walk, while we decided on a place to spend the night. We were aware of all the lodges and guest houses in the area, thanks to our extensive loitering around the town.

We finally got to a lodge and crashed, leaving poor Scotch to spend the night in a corner in the reception.

• • •

25

Scotch and the Pomeranians

Jan 8, 2014

It was my birthday. Probably the most unforgettable birthday of my life. I was glad we set out to look for the estate on my birthday. We marched out of our lodge early in the morning, our minds as confused as they were the previous day. Harish had called the previous night, and I had asked him to come to Adimaly.

Our first one hour was disappointing. But as the clock ticked past 7 a.m., something hit Nithin.

"Dude. Are you sure V.S. stands for Vineeth and Shruthi?" he asked.

"I don't know. You were the one who assumed that," I said.

"Okay. What are the other possibilities?"

I took a moment to think.

"Her dad's name is Victor. It could be what V stands for."

"Okay. What about S then? What is Vineeth's surname?" Nithin asked.

"Sengupta. His family name. That's an S. But we are still looking for fuckin 'V.S.'. What's your point here?" I asked.

"Wait. It was only the garment business for which they were partners right?"

"Maybe."

"Why should we even look for a V.S. then?" he asked.

"We should ask someone if there is an estate by the name Victor around."

We dispersed in different directions to ask as many people as possible. Most of us came back with negative answers. However, Sreedev and Vivek came back with similar stories.

"There was a Victor Coffee Estate a few kilometres uphill," Sreedev said.

"But they shut down business and sold the place years ago. Nothing is happening there right now," Vivek said.

"Yes. Perfect. Victor sold the estate to his partner, right?" Nithin asked, excited. "Does anyone recollect any name board that read Sengupta?"

"I remember a name board called Sen," Vivek said.

"Sen Estate?" I asked.

"No. Just Sen."

"Where?"

"At the dead end, we stopped last night. Scotch peed right under the name board," he said.

"Get in the car, guys," I said, excitedly and took the driver's seat.

• • •

We reached Sen estate. The board looked pretty old and worn out. The guys got out of the car and walked towards the gate. I took a moment to call Harish and inform him about the plan.

We put on our button cameras and walked through the gate. The estate was huge. There was a massive house about half a kilometre away from the gate. It had two storeys, with a green hip roof.

We heard the sound of dogs barking. Scotch got excited and began to respond to the barking and letting out loud growls in Rottweiler style. Vivek silenced him.

A huge, round figure walked out onto the balcony on the first floor of the house, hearing Scotch's barks.

"Vineeth," I gasped in triumph.

We charged into his house, before he could come out. We met him at the front door. He was taken aback by surprise when he saw us.

"Hi, Vineeth," I said.

"H-hiii," he said.

"I am Abhishek. The guy who loved your first ex-wife and who slept with your second," I said, attacking him head on.

I could see his face turning red. But he kept his temper down looking at the guys, who were all ready to pounce on him.

"Yeahhhh. Abi... Yes. Shruthi told me a lot about you. We also met once, right?" he said.

"What happened to Shruthi?" I asked, cutting right to the chase.

"S-sh she committed suicide," he said, in a low tone.

"Was it a suicide or a murder?" I asked, walking towards him, my eyes threatening to strangle him.

"M-M-Murder? What the fuck? Dude, you are crazy. How could..."

I stepped forward and held his neck before he spoke another word. I pinned him against the wall and held my fist up, all set to break his nose. With the mental state I was in, I would have chopped him into pieces.

"Abi. Give him a chance to speak," Chalu said.

I loosened my grip on his neck. The guys locked the door and carried him upstairs. They placed him on a chair. I took a chair too and sat right in front of him.

Vivek unfastened Scotch's collar. "Say hi to Scotch," I said.

"H-H-hii Scotch," he said, waving at him.

"Hey hey. Careful there. He hates people waving at him."

Vineeth put his hand down and sat as still as a statue.

"You know you've made a big mistake buying an estate at a dead end. You can only choose to run straight down that road there," I said, pointing in the direction of the gate.

"Why would I run?" he asked nervously.

"Because we might feel like breaking a tooth or two in case you don't give us the answers we want. But the best part here is that we wouldn't come after you if you choose to run. Scotch loves chasing, and he is specially trained to go for the balls first. Do you know how difficult it is to escape a Rottweiler's bite? And by the perfect placement of your hideout, there appears to be very meagre chances that you will find a vehicle to hop on before he tastes your flesh."

Vineeth looked at me and gulped in fright.

"I-I love dogs. I have a couple of Pomeranians in the room behind me," he said, trying to act friendly.

"So tell me. What happened to Shruthi?" I asked, ignoring his attempted amicability.

"S-she committed suicide," he said.

I stepped forward and slapped him with all the anger and frustration I had. He held his cheek and began to cry.

"It was really a suicide," he said, still crying. "I was in love with Shruthi from school but, she hated me.

During college, I learned that she was in love with you. So, I tried erasing her from my mind completely. But our dads were crazy. They had incessant quarrels over business. And it occurred to their stupid minds that the entire dispute would come to an end if they got us married. They didn't care about Shruthi's interests or bother about the huge difference in our religions and cultures. They cared about nothing but business.

Shruthi and I moved to Coimbatore after our wedding. We decided to keep away from our dads' business. We found jobs for ourselves. But our dads just did not let us live peacefully. Their difference in opinions in business continued.

Her dad tortured her to sign documents. He even hit her when she refused to. Ultimately, when she felt she couldn't take it anymore, she hung herself. My dad took this opportunity to file a few cases against him and put him in jail. Shruthi never loved me. We didn't even spend nights in the same bedroom. I felt terribly sorry for what she went through. I still am."

He continued to weep.

"And then you married Sushmita?" I asked.

"Yes."

"Why did you torture her?"

"Because I was a fucked up bastard. I yearned for love. So much that I began to get overly possessive. I behaved like a fucking psycho. I regret that. I really do."

"If you do, then why do you call her up every year and ask her cheap things?" I asked.

"That wasn't me. It was my dad. We sound similar over the phone. He is being stupid. He is trying to find evidence to convince her parents that she was the reason for the divorce. I even tried to call her a couple of times to apologise, but she never answered."

I looked at my friends. They looked at me with convinced faces. I stared at Vineeth, running the story through my mind again.

If Shruthi was in Coimbatore, why didn't she ever try to get in touch with me? I am sure she would have read the numerous emails I sent her.

"Why do I still feel you are cooking up a story?" I asked.

Vineeth looked at me without uttering a word. There was a moment of silence. The sound of a bark broke the hushed air. I heard the sound of scratching on a wooden wall behind Vineeth.

"Th-those are my Pomeranians. I guess they are hungry," he said.

I observed his hands. They were shaking. The scratching sound started from the bottom of the wall and slowly rose up to a height a Pomeranian could not reach. I frowned and stood up.

"You have a bigger dog back there?" I asked, my face showing my suspicion.

Vineeth smiled nervously. He slowly stood up.

"Yeah. Th-that's ummm..." He stepped forward, pushed me and sprinted downstairs.

We were all startled by this sudden unforeseen act.

"Scotch. Chase," Vivek screamed.

Scotch lifted his ears and leaped after him out of the room barking loudly. Vineeth sprinted out of the gate and ran down the road with Scotch close behind him. He was lucky enough to find a car at the end of the road. He stopped the car and jumped into it without even asking for permission. The car sped away. Scotch ran behind the car for some time and finally stopped.

Meanwhile, I sprinted towards the room from where the scratching sound was heard. The door was locked from outside. There was a Pomeranian outside the door that it looked at me with innocent eyes. I opened the door and stepped in.

It was dark. There were no windows or any kind of ventilation except a tiny gap in the ceiling. My hands ran over the walls searching for a light switch. I turned on all the switches that were available.

The room lit up with one too many lights. I adjusted my eyes to the brightness. I was startled by what I saw. Before me was a girl, who stood facing the wall, scribbling something on the wall with a piece of sharp wood. She did not bother to even react to the sound of the door opening or the lights being turned on. She continued to stand facing the wall, deeply involved in her scribbling. I took a few steps closer to her. She looked extremely emaciated and weak.

"Hello," I called out with anxiousness.

She did not respond.

She must be deaf. I thought.

"Can you hear me?" I asked, my voice growing louder.

No response. I took a few steps closer to her and observed what she was writing.

Happy Birthday, Abi. It read.

I was struck by realisation as soon as I read this. My heart beat so hard that it began to ache badly. I placed my shaking hand on her shoulder. She neither jumped because of my unexpected touch nor did she push my hand away. I slowly turned her around to see her face. I was shattered by what I saw.

"Shruthi???" I gasped, in complete disbelief.

Shruthi stared at me. Emotionless. She neither budged nor blinked an eye. She just kept staring at me as though she had no clue who I was.

I observed her face. She was as thin as a stick. Her skin had turned dark. She appeared so feeble that, I felt she would faint any moment.

"Abbiiiiiiiiiiiiiiiiiiiiiiiiii!" She began to wail loudly.

She fell on me. I held her and hugged her. She clutched me tightly and wailed uncontrollably. I looked at the room around me. It was a small room that had an attached bathroom. There was a tiny bed that had a table fan beside it. I observed the walls. It had the words 'Happy Birthday Abi' written all over.

My friends came running in as soon as they heard the sound of the wailing. They were staggered to see Shruthi. So was I. I just couldn't believe she was alive.

I was dismayed to see her physical state. It took me sometime to convince myself that it was all happening around me. But I did not cry. I tried to be strong. I wanted to give her all the emotional support that she needed. I held her close to me and just let her cry as much as she wanted.

• • •

26

Shruthi's Story

We called an ambulance and moved Shruthi to a hospital, where she underwent medical observation.

The doctor told us that she was physically fit, except that she was weak because of lack of nutrition. Her mental state was surprisingly stable, although she appeared a little disturbed by the harassment she would have possibly gone through. We were advised not to push her too much with questions until she was ready to talk about it.

"Sad that we couldn't catch Vineeth," Vivek said.

I smiled.

"We got him," I said.

"How do you know?"

"It was Harish's car that he dove into, to save himself from Scotch. That was my plan B. I put the idea of hopping into a vehicle that came his way into his head. He fell for it. Susheel must be dealing with him downhill."

"You called Susheel too?" he asked.

"Yes. Unofficially. After we provide him all the evidence, we'll leave it to them to decide what to do with him," I said.

"Perfect."

The nurse came out and told me that Shruthi wanted to see me. I walked into her hospital room, where she lay, taking glucose drips.

I looked at her state and felt extremely sorry. She looked at me and smiled, her dimples showing on her skinny cheeks. I sat beside her and held her hand. I kissed her forehead. My eyes welled up. She wiped my tears.

"Don't cry," she said. Her voice sounded weak.

"I thought you were dead," I said.

"They made it all up," she said.

"Who? Vineeth and his dad?"

She nodded.

"You remember the day I left for Idukki along with Vineeth to sign documents. He mixed some tablets in the water bottle I carried that made me unconscious. He undressed me and clicked pictures. He threatened that he would leak the pictures if I didn't marry him. I called you to Marrybrown to explain this to you. But he sent a few local goons before you arrived. They had a pistol. They threatened to shoot you if I did not ask you to leave immediately. He followed every move of mine."

"You could have told me this. I would have figured a way out. Or you could have at least gone to the police," I said.

"I tried as soon as you left. But those rowdies followed me all the way. Vineeth called me again and told me that he would kill you and my dad if I tried to inform the police.

He said he wouldn't have a problem going to jail. But he would make sure he killed both of you. I was completely helpless. That is why I sent you that break up SMS.

Meanwhile, there were heavy business disputes between our dads. His dad proposed to get me married to Vineeth and it happened. We got married in a hush-hush ceremony after which dad and grandma went abroad for a couple of years, in an attempt to build up his crashing business.

I decided to get in touch with you after the wedding and sort things out. But, soon after the wedding, Vineeth locked me up in a room in Coimbatore. I thought it was just going to be for a short while. But I was locked inside for thirty months, deprived of contact from the outside world. And he forced me to have sex with him almost every day."

"Didn't your dad try to get in touch with you?" I asked.

"Yes. But he did not let me speak to him. He kept lying to my dad that I was sleeping or having bath or outside or something like that. Meanwhile, more problems arose in the business. My dad came to India after about two-and-a-half years only to be arrested for a few cheque bounce cases that Vineeth's dad framed him for.

They also slapped a case of harassment on my father. They arranged an unclaimed body. A fake autopsy report and suicide note and made people believe that I was dead. My dad still thinks I am dead.

He buried the body in Coimbatore and moved me into Idukki where I had been locked up for three more years. These six years were hell for me Abi. I just had four walls around me to talk to. He was a psychotic bastard. All these years, I just sat there praying that I would be able to see you before I die."

"And the writing on the walls?" I asked.

"I wrote them. I did that every year. Even in the room in Coimbatore. I counted the days in my mind."

I had tears in my eyes. The amount of love she had for me was incomparable. In all the years, I had been longing to hear from her, she was undergoing hell in a locked room, with absolutely no hope before her. I just couldn't believe she experienced so much torture. I hugged her tightly and cried.

But she cried no more. She appeared to be relieved to talk to someone after so long. And I was glad it was I who found her. I did not want to stop her from speaking. I let her speak as much as she wanted.

• • •

We drove back to Coimbatore, our hearts filled with contentment. I was thrilled that my friends stood by me, helping me chase my gut right till the end. I put my arms around Shruthi, who sat with me in the front seat. She rested her head on my chest.

I thanked god for not letting us find the estate the previous day. If we did, we would have simply walked away convinced with Vineeth's story that he skillfully wove. I was thankful to my mom for giving birth to me on the 8th of January. I was grateful to Chalu for buying a new phone, which led to me sending the pictures accidentally to Sushmita.

Sushmita. Oh my God.

My heart jumped up and slapped me right on my head. What the hell was I going to tell her? I couldn't let go of Shruthi, but I definitely wouldn't be able to disappoint Sushmita either. I was in an absolute dilemma.

"Abi?" Shruthi said.

"Mmmmmm," I responded.

"I love you," she said, her head still rested on my chest.

Did she sense confusion in my mind? Was she asking me not to leave her? I held her closer to me and kissed her forehead.

"I love you too," I said.

• • •

We reached Renjith's house. Renjith had informed Jesse that we were coming, but did not tell her about Shruthi.

"Surprise!!!!" A group shouted as we walked in.

Other people from our college batch were there too. The place had been decorated with balloons and candles. There was a huge cake for me, which had the words 'Happy Birthday, Hero' on it. Beside the cake, stood another surprise. It was Sushmita. She had come straight to Renjith's house and arranged it all before we came.

Sushmita's eyes searched for me among the crowd. She found me walking in with my arms wrapped around Shruthi.

"Shruthi?" The women gasped, in astonishment.

They ran up to her. I looked at Sushmita. She shifted her glance between me and Shruthi. She mouthed the word Shruthi, looked at me and smiled. I could connect to that smile. It was a smile of worry. It was a smile that said that she appeared happy on the outside, but was worried on the inside. She came up to me.

"Sushmita. I-I..."

She placed her hand on my mouth.

"You don't have to explain..." She brushed my hair and walked into the bedroom.

She had turned her back to me, but I could feel tears running down her cheeks. Everybody remained silent and confused. I had to talk to her. I held Shruthi's hand and followed Sushmita into the bedroom.

She was seated on her bed, holding her face, crying. I sat on the bed and placed my hand around her shoulders. She tilted her head to me and continued to cry. I remained silent, as I did not know what to tell her. Shruthi appeared confused. I waited for Sushmita to compose herself and then I looked at Shruthi.

"Shruthi, this is Sushmita, my..."

"Friend," Sushmita said, interrupting me.

I looked at her. She did not look at me. She looked at Shruthi instead.

"Shruthi. You and I married the same guy. We also fell in love with the same guy," Sushmita said.

Shruthi looked at me.

"Are you both in love?" she asked, ignoring the 'married to one guy' part.

I could see the worry on her face. She did not go to the extent of thinking I would be in another relationship.

"Abi, I'm sorry, I did not realise that you..." She began to weep. "I am a complete idiot," she said, trying to push the words through her tears. "How could I ever presume that you would still be thinking of me?"

I looked at Sushmita and then back at her.

"Shruthi. I.. I..."

"Why did you come find me, Abi? I would have spent the rest of my life in that room thinking about you." She took a moment to catch her breath.

"You have been my only world, Abi. I am just not able to digest the fact that my world belongs to someone else."

She wailed loudly. She obviously could not think past me. She had seen absolutely nothing in her life for the past six years. I stepped forward and hugged her. She clutched me tightly and buried her face into my chest, breaking down miserably."

I remained silent. I did not know what to say to console her. There was an awkward moment of silence.

"Shruthi, Abi is not in love with me. I am in love with him," Sushmita said, breaking the silence. "I thought he would accept my love some day. But I don't think it will ever happen."

I looked at Sushmita, startled by what she said. She mouthed the words "it's okay" to me. I felt miserable but did not utter a word. I just did not know what to tell. Sushmita held my hand.

"Happy birthday, Abi," she said.

I love you, Sushmita, I said in my mind.

"I'm going to let you guys talk for a while. Let's celebrate your birthday as soon as you are done," she said and walked away, wiping away her tears.

The guys drank and rejoiced. Sushmita tried her best to keep herself happy, but couldn't help the pain that descended upon her. Shruthi remained cuddled close to me all night. I felt really really sorry for Sushmita.

• • •

I was driving Sushmita to the airport the next day. I had narrated to her all that Shruthi went through. She was totally shocked.

"She needs you, Abi," she said.

"I am sorry," I said.

"You don't have to be. This is a sacrifice that you and I have to make. For her. I know how insane Vineeth can get and by what you said, I am sure she would have gone through a lot of torture. She cannot bear losing you, Abi. It was for you that she kept herself alive all these years. You have to be there for her."

"But I know you are hiding all the pain. Your eyes say it all."

"I was, Abi. I still might be. But I thought about it deeply last night. I will be able to get over you. I am going to London in a couple of weeks time. I will soon be lost in a world of my own," she said.

I drove to the airport and stopped at the entrance. "Is this the last time we see each other?" I asked.

"Maybe. Maybe not. Let time decide that."

I nodded hesitantly. She glanced at me. I took a final look at her fish-shaped eyes. She leaned forward, gave me a hug and kissed me on my cheek.

"Bye, hero," she whispered into my ear.

She collected her bag and got out of the car, into the airport. I stared at her as she walked away. I could see her wiping away her tears. My eyes welled up too.

"Buhbye, Sushmita Banerjee," I said with my voice breaking. I drove away with a heavy heart. I knew it would take some time for the scale of these events to sink into me. As Sushmita said, we had to make this sacrifice for Shruthi.

27

A Beginning

Five Months Later

"Cut," Renjith screamed through the megaphone.

I wiped away my tears. Sushmita turned around and laughed. They were at an airport set, enacting the last shot of the entire movie.

"Did I overact?" she asked.

"No, it was perfect," Renjith said.

"You are an amazing actor," I told Sushmita.

"You can stop pretending to scratch my back, Abi. The schedule is done." Sushmita said.

I laughed.

"And that's pack-up. Wrap-up. Whatever you want to call it. Shoot's over. Thank you all for the support. Let's get the fuck out of here and drink until our eyeballs fall out," Renjith announced through the mike.

"Some bytes for the media before you even think of that," our PR said.

"Oh yeah. I almost forgot," Renjith said.

• • •

Director Renjith, cinematographer Manjunath and actors Abhishek, Shreya Gupta and Sushmita Banerjee, we all took turns answering questions in individual interviews the people from different media took.

"We heard that you had been through a lot of struggle before you got this big break. Can you tell us what kept you going?" VJ Abishek from Behindwoods asked.

I smiled and looked at a magic smiley tattooed in my hand.

"It is this magic smiley," I said. "I would like to quote what my college lecturer once told me. The world outside is not going to be a walk on the moon. You will be washed, battered, wrung and put out to dry. It is the character in you that will help you withstand difficult situations. My wife drew this magic smiley on my hand when we first met."

I took a moment to reminisce the moment.

"She told me that the magic smiley would help me get what I wanted and it worked only if I smiled. I don't know how serious she was, but I see the philosophy in it. No matter how disastrous life can get, if you believe in what you want and face your problems with a smile on your face, you will ultimately get there."

"That's a lovely thought," VJ Abishek said. "Can you tell us a little about your journey? We heard an interesting titbit that, Sushmita, one of the female leads in the movie is your friend. What made you zero in on her?"

Sushmita... She was a poetically beautiful book that needed special privileges to open. I smiled. There were tones of memories behind that smile.

"I like narrating my stories in detail. Are you okay with that?" I asked.

www.ingramcontent.com/pod-product-compliance
Lightning Source LLC
LaVergne TN
LVHW042343150826
845671LV00001B/2

* 9 7 9 8 8 9 4 7 5 9 1 9 7 *